lhasa ap

C000000974

understanding and
caring for your breed

Written by
Patricia Conlon

lhasa apso

understanding and
caring for your breed

Written by
Patricia Conlon

pet book publishing

Pet Book Publishing Company

The Old Hen House St Martin's Farm, Zeals,
Warminster, Wiltshire BA12 6NZ

Printed by Printworks Global Ltd, London & Hong Kong

ISBN: 978-1-910488-40-9

Contents

Introducing the Lhasa Apso

The Lhasa Apso is one of the most captivating of breeds. Jaunty and full of self-importance, he belies his small size with his big personality. In the looks department, he is a real stunner and will turn heads wherever he goes.

Physical characteristics

The exotic looking Lhasa Apso is a natural in the show ring but, in fact, his appearance is dictated by purely practical concerns.

This little dog comes from the mountains of Tibet, a land that is known for its extreme temperatures, rough terrain and bright sunlight. In the space of a day, temperatures can range from below zero to 38 degrees Celsius (100 F), and in the north and west of the country temperatures can drop to minus 40 degrees Celsius (-40 F).

The Lhasa Apso has a long, luxuriant coat which is hard in texture; a woolly coat or a silky coat would not provide adequate protection for the demanding environment of his homeland. He also an undercoat for extra insulation.

The head fall – the hair on the head that comes down over the eyes – looks highly impractical but, in reality, it serves a very useful purpose.

In Tibet the sunlight is incredibly bright, and the glare from the white snow is intense, so the head fall offers a form of sunscreen. In addition, the Lhasa has long eyelashes which keep the hair out of his eyes, thereby protecting them from injury.

In terms of conformation, the Lhasa Apso is small but sturdy; he is a long way removed from the fine-boned Toy breeds that struggle to withstand the rigours of everyday life. Living at the high altitudes of Tibet, adequate heart and lung space was essential. He therefore has well-sprung ribs, extending well back to a strong loin

The Lhasa has a short muzzle, and is therefore termed a partial-brachycephalic breed. Although the foreface is foreshortened, it as not as exaggerated as is the case with the true brachycephalic breeds, such as the Pug and the Pekingese.

As a result he does not suffer the attendant respiratory problems that can be associated with this conformation. His head is framed by heavily feathered ears, and this, along with his dark, oval-shaped eyes, gives him a somewhat human appearance.

This is a dog that is longer than he is tall; a sense of balance is created with the head joined to an arched neck, a relatively long back topped with a well-feathered tail that is carried over the back.

Bred to live in the extreme climate of Tibet, the Lhasa Apso is a surprisingly sturdy little dog.

The Lhasa Apso comes in a wonderful range of colours, with or without white markings, and so you are bound to find something that suits your personal preference.

Temperament

The Lhasa Apso is distinctive in looks – and he is matchless in personality. He is a charming mixture of parts, and although there are Lhasa traits to look for, each dog will have his own, unique temperament.

The Breed Standard (see What should a Lhasa Apso look like) has a written description of the Lhasa character, and it is worth looking at the terminology in more detail:

"Gay": This is the perfect adjective to describe the high-spirited temperament of this little dog who has a tremendous sense of fun.

"Assertive": Everything about the Lhasa Apso says: "look at me, take notice of me". He has total belief in his own self-importance and woe betide anyone who puts him in second place!

"Alert": The Lhasa is quick-witted and clever; he likes to be part of everything that is going on and will sound a warning at the least excuse.

"Steady": The Lhasa Apso is sound in temperament and extremes of behaviour are untypical.

"Aloof/chary with strangers": The Lhasa is a perfect companion dog but, as far as he is concerned, there is a dividing line between his beloved family and friends, and people he doesn't know. There is no hint of aggression in his make up, but he will not rush up and greet people he doesn't know. Neither will he appreciate being forced into interactions; he prefers to make his own decisions and this should always be respected.

In terms of training, the Lhasa is as bright as a button but he has no time for monotonous drilling and will quickly cease to co-operate if there are no tangible rewards on offer. The key to Lhasa training is to make it all a game, reinforcing the behaviour you want by giving praise and food treats, while always remembering to quit while you are ahead.

The perfect home

When you take on a Lhasa Apso, your home will be transformed. He may be a small dog, but his personality will brim over. He will provide entertainment; the Lhasa has a great sense of fun and he certainly seems to have his own quirky sense of humour.

He is loving and affectionate and will enjoy no end of cuddles; he will also keep you on your toes, giving a warning bark (or a series of barks...) to let you know when strangers are approaching.

Town or country, apartment or mansion, the Lhasa Apso is infinitely adaptable, as long as he is given lots of attention and is included in family activities.

Interestingly, the Lhasa does not shed his coat, which makes him a good choice for allergy sufferers. However if you or a member of your family has an allergy, it is advisable to spend some time with the breed before making a commitment. In some cases, the allergy relates to the dandruff (dander) rather than to the hair itself.

The Lhasa Apso is relatively easy to care for but think long and hard about how you are going to cope with his long coat. Keeping a Lhasa in full coat requires a huge amount of dedication which is why the majority of owners opt for a puppy/pet trim.

We are fortunate that the Lhasa is a long-lived breed, and once your puppy has matured, you can look forward to many years of companionship with this most endearing of dogs.

Facing page: The adaptable Lhasa will fit into a variety of lifestyles.

Tracing back in time

The Lhasa Apso has a fascinating history, seeped in the myths and legends of Tibetan Buddhism. No wonder this little dog has such an air of importance!

The Lhasa Apso is an ancient breed; some claim it dates back to 800 BC, but as Tibet's first written records start in AD 639, this cannot be substantiated. However, we do know that Buddhism spread into Tibet from India in the 7th century, so this is where our story starts.

The lion is a powerful figure in Buddhist mythology and the Lhasa Apso is known as the little lion dog. Buddha Manjusri, the god of learning, reputedly travelled round as a simple priest, accompanied by his dog. When he needed to travel long distances, the dog would transform into a lion, so the Buddha could ride on his back.

The Lhasa is also associated with the snow lion who had such power that, with a single roar, seven dragons fell out of the sky.

Sacred watch dogs

As Buddhism became established in Tibet, monasteries were built as religious centres and as home for the Buddhist monks. Large guard dogs – Tibetan Mastiffs – protected the monasteries from intruders. But if anyone got past these ferocious dogs, there was back up in the form of the Lhasa Apso.

These short-legged dogs, probably descended from European herding dogs, such as the Puli and Pumi, were highly valued as watch dogs. Alert and intelligent, the Lhasa Apso would be ready to give a warning bark if strangers were approaching.

Naming the breed

The Lhasa Apso has a highly distinctive name but what does it mean? In Tibet, the word 'Apso' refers to any long-coated dog, although it is generally associated with small dogs. The Lhasa Apso was also called by another name, 'Apso Seng Kyi', which translates as 'Bark Sentinel Lion Dog' – a clear reference to the breed's place as a sacred watch dog.

Gift dogs

The Tibetans have always held their dogs in high esteem, and the Lhasa Apso became the favoured watch dog and companion for the wealthy families of Tibet. Members of the nobility and merchants kept Lhasa Apsos to guard their homes and their valuables.

In Tibetan culture, it was unheard of to sell a dog. However, they were presented as gifts, often as a talisman to ensure safe passage for merchants travelling from Tibet to China – a journey that took some 10 months to complete.

The Dalai Lama had a custom of presenting Lhasa Apsos as bringers of good fortune, and it is known that these little dogs were given as gifts to the imperial families of China.

As favoured dogs, Lhasa Apsos were given the best of care and jealously guarded as the most prized of possessions.

Owners were very reluctant to part with their dogs, so it is little wonder that the breed remained a well-kept secret for many centuries before it was discovered by the western world.

Developing the breed

The first Lhasa Apsos reached the west in the late 19th century, but it took some decades before they were established as a recognised breed.

There are stories of Lhasa Apsos arriving in England in the latter half of the 19th century, mostly imported by the Hon Mrs McLaren-Morrison who specialised in importing foreign breeds. One dog, known as Bhutan, made a name for himself as a fund-raiser, begging to raise money at dog shows.

However as more dogs made the journey from Tibet, there was growing confusion about the different breeds that came from this part of the world. In 1934 the Tibetan Breeds Association was established in the UK with the aim of drawing a distinction between the breeds.

Breed pioneers including Mrs Irma Bailey, who spent some time in Tibet, and Lady Freda Valentine

set down the 'ideals' of the dogs that were being imported. Their conclusion was that there were four distinct Tibetan breeds: the Lhasa Apso, the Tibetan Spaniel, the Tibetan Terrier and the Tibetan Mastiff.

The Shih Tzu, whose roots are also Chinese, was classified as a separate breed. A brief overview of the breeds highlights their distinct appearances:

Lhasa Apso: A long-coated dog that is well balanced in build, and longer than he is tall. The head-shape, with foreshortened muzzle is a breed feature. His temperament – friendly and gay, but wary of strangers – is unique to the breed.

Tibetan Terrier: A long-coated breed but substantially bigger than the Lhasa Apso, with a square outline and a much longer foreface. Despite the obvious difference between the two breeds, there were many cases of mistaken identity and for a time there were classes for dogs known as Lhasa Terriers.

Tibetan Spaniel: This little dog, which is roughly the same size as a Lhasa Apso, was more easily recognised as a pure breed. A typical Tibetan Spaniel has a shorter coat with smooth hair on his face. The skull is domed, and the forelegs are slightly bowed, which gives him a markedly different appearance.

Tibetan Mastiff: As already noted, this is a large and powerful dog, standing at least 66cm (26in) at the shoulder. His thick coat is black and tan, black or red. In his native home, he was used to guard the flock and to act as a watch dog.

Shi Tzu: Often confused with the Lhasa Apso, the Shih Tzu has roots in China and Tibet. Outwardly the two breeds bear a strong resemblance to each other, but there are important differences. The Shih Tzu has a different shaped head (broad, round and wide between the eyes), and he is far more out-going and amenable that the Lhasa, who takes time to welcome strangers.

It takes an expert eye to differentiate the Lhasa and the Shih Tzu (pictured).

The Lhasa in America

The first two Lhasa Apsos arrived in the USA in 1933; the 13th Dalai Lama presented them to breed enthusiasts, Mr and Mrs Suydam Cutting. They had been in touch with Lhasa breeder, Irma Bailey, in the UK and as a result they set up a correspondence with His Holiness which resulted in his gift. In return they presented him with two Dalmatians and two German Hounds. Over the ensuing decades more dogs were imported but, again confusion reigned over the identity of the Shih Tzu and the Lhasa Apso and there was much inter-breeding. Fortunately some lines remained pure and by the 1950s the two breeds had gained official recognition.

The current era

Today, the Lhasa Apso is established worldwide as a show dog and as a companion. Eclipsed in numbers by the more popular Shih Tzu, the Lhasa Apso has its own devoted following. In the show ring, breeders are striving to produce the very best specimens that are true to the Breed Standard and entirely typical of this very special breed. But, perhaps more importantly, the Lhasa Apso is valued as the most wonderful companion dog. Beautiful to look at, ever alert, he will watch over your home and family and give you his undivided love and affection.

The Lhasa Apso has an enthusiastic worldwide fan club.

What should a Lhasa Apso look like?

The Lhasa Apso, with his flowing coat and jaunty air draws admiring glances wherever he goes. So what makes a Lhasa so special?

The aim of breeders is to produce dogs that are sound, healthy, typical examples of their chosen breed, in terms of both looks and temperament. To achieve this, they are guided by a Breed Standard, which is a written blueprint describing the perfect specimen.

Of course, there is no such thing as a 'perfect' dog, but breeders aspire to produce dogs that conform as closely as possible to the picture in words presented by the Breed Standard. In the show ring, judges use the Breed Standard to assess the dogs that come before them, and it is the dog that, in their opinion, comes closest to the ideal, that will win top honours.

This has significance beyond the sport of showing, for it is the dogs that win in the ring which will be used for breeding. The winners of today are therefore responsible for passing on their genes to future generations and preserving the breed in its best form.

There are some differences in the wording of the Breed Standard depending on national kennel clubs; the American Kennel Club and the Federation Cynologique Internationale, which is the governing body for 86 countries, have far more descriptive Standards than the brief outline given in the English version.

General appearance

The Lhasa Apso is a well-balanced, sturdy dog. Despite his small stature, he is solid in build.

Temperament

This is a gay little dog with an air of self-importance. He tends to be wary of strangers.

Head

The head has heavy furnishings with a good fall of hair over the eyes and a long beard. In terms of shape, the skull is narrow. The American Standard describes the head by stating what it not desirable, i.e. "not quite flat, but not domed or apple-shaped". The muzzle is of medium length (approx 4cm/1.5in); the American states that a square muzzle is "objectionable". The nose is black.

Eyes

When a Lhasa Apso is in full coat, his eyes are obscured, but they should be dark brown in colour, medium-sized, neither sunken nor protruding. Again the American Standard describes the eyes in terms of negatives, i.e. "neither very large and full, nor very small and sunk". The English Standard stipulates that there should be no white showing at the top or the base of the eye.

Ears

The shape of the ears is not visible because of the head fall but they are low-set, pendulous and heavily feathered.

Mouth

The English and FCI Standards ask for a reverse scissor bite, which means the upper incisors close just inside the incisors on the lower jaw.

The American Standard uses different terminology, saying the bite can be slightly undershot or level, which is where the incisors meet tip to tip.

Dogs with narrow muzzles may have missing teeth; the English and FCI Standards emphasise that full dentition is desirable.

Neck

This should be strong and well arched. It is covered with a mane of hair, which is more pronounced in males.

Forequarters

The shoulders are well laid back; the forelegs are straight and heavily furnished with hair.

The Lhasa Apso carries himself with an air of self-importance.

Body

The length of the body from the shoulders to the buttocks should be longer than the height at the withers (the highest point of the shoulders).

The topline is level and the compact body should be well ribbed with a strong loin. The overall appearance should be balanced.

Hindquarters

The hindquarters should be muscled and well developed which contributes to the Lhasa's sturdy appearance.

Underneath the hair furnishings, there should be good angulation. Viewed from the rear, the hocks ('ankles') should be parallel and not too close together.

Feet

The feet are round and cat-like with good pads. They are well feathered.

Tail

The tail, which is well feathered, is carried over the back in a screw – but not like a pot-hook. A kink at the end of the tail is acceptable but a low-set tail is considered a serious fault.

Coat

The Lhasa's coat is his most striking feature. It should be heavy, straight and hard to the touch; a silky or woolly coat is incorrect. The coat should be of good length, reaching to the floor but not impeding movement.

The head-fall should go over the eyes, but should not obscure vision. There should be a good set of whiskers and a beard.

The Lhasa has a "moderate" undercoat according to the English Standard; it was formerly described as "dense", a term still used in the FCI Standard.

The undercoat was needed to provide much-needed insulation in the harsh climate of the Lhasa's Tibetan home, so "dense" might be a more fitting description.

Colour

The Lhasa Apso comes in a wonderful variety of colours, and all are equally acceptable. They include: golden, sandy, honey, dark grizzle, slate, smoke, parti-coloured (white with a solid colour), black, white or brown.

On lighter coloured dogs, the hair on the ears and beard may have dark tips.

Movement

This is described as "free and jaunty" which indicates the style of movement rather than a specific gait. However, the correct conformation – a body that is longer than it is high, well laid shoulders and closely fitting elbows – should allow a smooth, flowing action.

Size

The English and FCI Standards go for an ideal height of 25cm (10 in) for males; females are slightly smaller. The American Standard states that size is "variable" but recommends that males should be 25-28cm (10 or 11in) at the withers and females should be slightly smaller.

Summing up

Although the majority of Lhasa Apsos are kept as pet dogs and will never be exhibited in the show ring, it is important that breeders strive for perfection and try to produce dogs that adhere as closely as possible to the Breed Standard.

This is the best way of ensuring that the Lhasa Apso remains sound in mind and body, and retains the characteristics that are unique to this very special breed.

Facing page: The glamorous coat is the Lhasa's crowning glory.

What do you want from your Lhasa?

There are over 200 dog breeds to choose from, so how can you be sure that the Lhasa Apso is the right breed for you? Before you decide on a Lhasa you need to be 100 per cent confident that this is the breed that is best suited to your lifestyle.

Companion

The Lhasa Apso is one of the most companionable of all breeds, bringing his own unique personality to his role as a devoted family dog. He has an untroubled outlook on life and his optimistic, mischievous nature is a source of endless entertainment.

However he is reserved with strangers, and this trait needs to be managed so he never feels the need to escalate his behaviour.

This is a dog that fits in with a variety of lifestyles; he is suitably robust to enjoy the hurly burly of family life and although he enjoys exercise, his requirements are moderate so he will be happy living with older owners.

He is a most affectionate dog but he will generally find the antics of toddlers are a little too much for him and will prefer living with older children.

Sports dog

If you are interested in getting involved in canine sports, a Lhasa Apso would not be your first choice. There is no doubting his intelligence, but he is not a naturally obedient dog, and although he can move swiftly when he wants to, he is not a born athlete.

However, there are options which will suit a Lhasa if you enjoy training – so don't write him off! See Opportunities for Lhasas.

Show dog

Do you have ambitions to exhibit your Lhasa Apso in the show ring? The Lhasa is a most glamorous breed, and he enjoys showing off. However, you need to have a passion for grooming because keeping a Lhasa in full coat is no easy matter.

If you plan to show your Lhasa Apso you need to

track down a show quality puppy, and train him so he will perform in the ring, and accept the detailed 'hands on' examination which is part of the judging process. It is also important to bear in mind that not every puppy with show potential develops into a top quality specimen, and so you must be prepared to love your Lhasa and give him a home for life, even if he doesn't make the grade.

If you plan to exhibit your Lhasa, you will need to find a breeder that specialises in producing show quality dogs.

What does your Lhasa want from you?

A dog cannot speak for himself, so we need to view the world from a canine perspective and work out what a Lhasa Apso needs in order to live a happy, contented and fulfilling life.

Time and commitment

First of all, a Lhasa Apso needs a commitment that you will care for him for the duration of his life, guiding him through his puppyhood, enjoying his adulthood, and being there for him in his later years.

If all potential owners were prepared to make this pledge, there would be scarcely any dogs in rescue. The Lhasa is a superb companion dog, but he does not come readymade.

You need to take charge of his education, guiding him through puppyhood and adolescence, so that he understands his place in the family. He is an active, out-going dog and he will be thoroughly miserable if he is excluded from family activities or expected to spend lengthy periods on his own.

It is important that all dogs can cope with spending some time on their own so they don't become anxious, but the maximum time a dog should be left is four hours.

If this does not fit in with your lifestyle, you should delay owning a dog until your circumstances change.

Practical matters

The Lhasa Apso is a fairly sturdy little dog and does not need special care in day-to-day life, but his coat is a consideration. You have two options: keeping him in full coat, which is a massive undertaking, or opting for a puppy/pet trim.

This looks smart and is much easier to maintain but you will need to employ the services of a groomer as well as keeping the coat in good order on a daily basis.

This is not a chore if you enjoy grooming, but you need to have the time to devote to it.The Lhasa Apso is infinitely adaptable when it comes to exercise.

He will accompany his family on long rambles and he will be content to go on shorter expeditions as long as he has access to a garden.

Remember mental stimulation is as important as physical exercise, so if he is more of a home dog, he needs to be included in all that is going on so that his brain is fully occupied.

Leadership

The Lhasa Apso is not a challenging breed and, with the right guidance, he will find his place in the family and become the perfect companion.

It is your job to show your Lhasa how you want him to behave by rewarding the behaviour that you consider desirable. You need to be 100 per cent consistent, so he is left in no doubt as to what is deemed acceptable.

If you are over-indulgent and treat him like a baby, he will not thrive. His relationship with you will be confused and he may become over-dependant.

This is not a good situation for him, or for you, as he will become anxious and stressed if he is asked to cope on his own.

All this can be avoided by giving him clear guidelines. See Settling in.

Extra considerations

Now you have decided that a Lhasa Apso is the dog of your dreams, you can narrow your choice so you know exactly what you are looking for.

Male or female?

The choice of male or female Lhasa Apso comes down to personal preference. Males are slightly bigger than females, and they may have a more luxuriant coat. In terms of temperament, all Lhasas are individuals but as a generalisation, males tend to be more affectionate. Females can be slightly aloof but when they bestow their affection, it is a gift indeed...

If you opt for a female, you will need to cope with her seasons, which will start at any time between 6-12 months of age and occur approximately every nine months thereafter.

During the three-week period of a season, you will need to keep your bitch away from entire males (males that have not been neutered) to eliminate the risk of an unwanted pregnancy. Some owners also report that females may be a little moody and withdrawn during their seasonal cycle.

Many pet owners opt for neutering, which puts an end to the seasons, and also has many attendant health benefits. The operation, known as spaying, is usually carried out at some point after the first season. The best plan is to seek advice from your vet.

The male Lhasa is slow to mature; he may not settle down until he is three to four years of age. You will need to make the decision whether to neuter your male or leave him entire. An entire male may not cause many problems, although some do have a stronger tendency to mark, which could include inside the house.

However, training will usually put a stop to this. An entire male will also be on the lookout for bitches in season, and this may lead to difficulties, depending on your circumstances.Neutering (castrating) a male is a relatively simple operation, and there are associated health benefits. Again, you should seek advice from your vet.

Colour

There is a wonderful variety of colours to choose from. These include:

Pale cream ranging through all shades of gold

Black (if the skin is blue, the dog is a true black, otherwise the coat will lighten to grey)

Silver sables

Gold sables

Brown

White

Slate

Grizzle (mixed colours within the hairs)

Particolour (white with a solid colour)

All colours are equally acceptable in the show ring, so it all comes down to what you prefer...

More than one?

Owning a Lhasa Apso is highly addictive and you may want to expand your canine population. Owning a mini tribe will bring great pleasure to you – and your dogs will enjoy each other's company – but you need to get your timing right.

Be wary of a breeder who encourages you to buy two puppies from the same litter, as it is unlikely that the welfare of the puppies is their top priority. Pups of the same or similar ages will bond with each other rather than with you – and they will get up to all sorts of mischief.

If you get two puppies of a similar age they will be more than twice the trouble.

Most responsible breeders have a waiting list of potential purchasers before a litter is even born and have no need to make this type of sale.

If you do decide to take on a second Lhasa Apso, wait at least 18 months so your first dog is fully trained and settled before embarking on a puppy. In terms of gender combination, two males may be competitive, particularly if they are entire. Females do get on well together, but there may be the occasional falling out. The best combination is a male/female pair but obviously you will need to neuter one or both dogs if they are living together.

Taking on an older dog

You may decide to miss out on the puppy phase and take on an older dog instead. Such a dog may be harder to track down, but sometimes a breeder may have a youngster that is not suitable for showing, but is perfect for a family pet.

In some cases, a breeder may rehome a female when her breeding career is at an end so she can enjoy the benefits of more individual attention. There are advantages to taking on an older dog, as you know exactly what you are getting. But the upheaval of changing homes can be quite upsetting, so you will need to have plenty of patience during the settling in period.

Rehoming a rescued dog

We are fortunate that the number of Lhasas that end up in rescue is relatively small. However, there are a number of dogs that need rehoming through no fault of their own. The reasons are various, ranging from illness or death of the original owner to family breakdown, changing jobs, or even the arrival of a new baby.

You are unlikely to find a Lhasa Apso in an all-breed rescue centre; contacting a specialist breed club that runs a rescue scheme will be your best option if you decide to go down this route. Try to find out as much as you can about the dog's history so you know exactly what you are taking on. You need to be aware of age and health status, likes and dislikes, plus any behavioural issues that may be relevant.

You need to be realistic about what you are capable of achieving so you can be sure you can give the dog in question a permanent home.

Regardless of the dog's previous history, you will need to give him plenty of time and be patient with him as he settles into his new home. It may take weeks, or even months before he becomes fully integrated in the family, but if all goes well you will have the reward of knowing that you have provided a forever home.

Sourcing a puppy

> Your aim is to find a healthy puppy that is typical of the breed, and has been reared with the greatest possible care. Where do you start?

A tried and trusted method of finding a puppy is to attend a dog show where your chosen breed is being exhibited. This will give you the opportunity to see lots of different Lhasa Apsos of all ages and in a variety of colours. To begin with, you may think that colour is the only difference between the individual dogs but when you look closely you will detect that there are different 'types' on show.

They are all purebred Lhasa Apsos, but breeders produce dogs with a family likeness, so you can see which type you prefer. When judging has been completed, talk to the exhibitors and find out more about their dogs. They may not have puppies available, but some will be planning a litter, and you may decide to put your name on a waiting list.

Internet research

The Internet is an excellent resource, but when it comes to finding a puppy, use it with care:

DO go to the website of your national kennel club.

Both the American Kennel Club (AKC) and the Kennel Club (KC) have excellent websites which will give you information about the Lhasa Apso as a breed, and what to look for when choosing a puppy. You will also find contact details for specialist breed clubs (see below). Both sites have lists of puppies available, and you can look out for breeders of merit (AKC) and assured breeders (KC) which indicate that a code of conduct has been adhered to.

DO find details of specialist breed clubs.

On breed club websites you will find lots of useful information which will help you to care for your Lhasa. There may be contact details of breeders in your area, or you may need to go through the club secretary. Some websites also have a list of breeders that have puppies available. The advantage of going through a breed club is that members will follow a code of ethics, and this will give you some guarantees regarding breeding stock and health checks.

If you are planning to show your Lhasa Apso you should obviously go to a breeder that has had some success in the ring, so you will need to do additional research to discover more about their breeding lines and the type of Lhasa they produce.

DO NOT look at puppies for sale.

There are legitimate Lhasa Apso breeders with their own websites, and they may, occasionally, advertise a litter, although in most cases reputable breeders have waiting lists for their puppies. The danger comes from unscrupulous breeders that produce puppies purely for profit, with no thought for the health of the dogs they breed from and no care given to rearing the litter. Photos of puppies are hard to resist, but never make a decision based purely on an advertisement. You need to find out who the breeder is, and have the opportunity to visit their premises and inspect the litter before making a decision.

Questions, questions, questions

When you find a breeder with puppies available, you will have lots of questions to ask. These should include the following:

- Where have the puppies been reared? They should have been cared for in a home environment which gives them the best possible start in life.

- How many are in the litter?

- What is the split of males and females?

- What colours are available?

- How many have already been spoken for? The breeder will probably be keeping a puppy to show

Facing page: The breeder will quiz you to find out if you can provide a suitable home for a Lhasa puppy.

or for breeding, and there may be others on a waiting list.

- Can I see the mother with her puppies?

- What age are the puppies?

- When will they be ready to go to their new homes?

Bear in mind puppies need to be with their mother and siblings until they are at least eight weeks of age otherwise they miss out on vital learning and communication skills, which will have a detrimental effect on them for the rest of their lives.

Many Lhasa breeders prefer to wait until the pups are 10 weeks old before letting them go to their new homes, when they are better able to cope with the transition.

You should also be prepared to answer a number of searching questions so the breeder can check if you are suitable as a potential owner for one of their precious puppies.

You will be asked some or all of the following questions:

- What is your home set up?

- Do you have children/grandchildren?

- What are their ages?

- Do you have a securely fenced garden?

- Is there somebody at home the majority of the time?

- What is your previous experience with dogs?

- Do you already have other dogs at home?

- Do you have plans to show your Lhasa Apso?

The breeder is not being intrusive; they just need to understand the type of home you will be able to provide in order to make the right match. Do not be offended by this; the breeder is doing it both for your, and the dog's, benefit.

Steer clear of a breeder who does not ask you questions. He or she may be more interested in making money out of the puppies than ensuring that they go to good homes. They may also have taken other shortcuts which may prove disastrous, and very expensive, in terms of vet bills or plain heartache.

Health issues

In common with all pure-bred dogs, the Lhasa Apso suffers from some hereditary problems so you need to talk to the breeder about the health status of breeding stock and find out if there are any issues of concern.

Puppy watching

Who can resist a litter of Lhasa puppies running and tumbling towards you? You will probably want to take the whole lot home with you! However, you must not let your heart rule your head. Try to put your feelings to one side so that you can make an informed choice.

You need to be 100 per cent confident that the breeding stock is healthy, and the puppies have been reared with love and care, before making a commitment to buy.

Viewing a litter

It is a good idea to have a mental checklist of what to look out for when you visit a breeder. You want to see:

- A clean, hygienic environment.

- Puppies who are out-going, friendly, and eager to meet you.

- A sweet-natured mother who is ready to show off her pups.

- Puppies that are well covered, but not pot-bellied, which could be an indication of worms.

- Bright eyes, with no sign of soreness or discharge.

- Clean ears that smell fresh.

- No discharge from the ears or the nose.

- Clean rear ends – matting could indicate an upset tummy.

It is important that you see the mother with her puppies as this will give you a good idea of the temperament they are likely to inherit. It is also helpful if you can meet other close relatives so you can see the type of Lhasa the breeder produces.

In most cases, you will not be able to see the father (sire) as most breeders will travel some distance to find a stud dog that is not too close to their own bloodlines and complements their bitch.

However, you should be able to see photos of him and be given the chance to examine his pedigree and show record.

Companion puppy

If you are looking for a Lhasa purely as a companion, you should be guided by the breeder who will have spent hours and hours puppy watching, and will know each of the pups as an individual.

It is tempting to choose a puppy yourself, but the breeder will take into account your family set up and lifestyle and will help you pick the most suitable puppy.

Show puppy

If you are buying a puppy with the hope of showing him, make sure you make this clear to the breeder. A lot of planning goes into producing a litter, and although all the puppies will have been reared with equal care, there will be one or two that have show potential.

Ideally, recruit a breed expert to inspect the puppies with you so you have the benefit of their objective evaluation. The breeder will also be there to help as they will want to ensure that only the best of their stock is exhibited in the show ring.

Wait until the puppies are between seven and eight weeks before making your choice as this gives them time to develop.

It is impossible to say with certainty that a puppy

is going to be successful in the show ring; puppies go through many stages when they are growing and the ugly duckling could well surprise you. However, there are certain guidelines which are worth following:

Despite his small size, a Lhasa puppy should be the correct shape, i.e. the length of his body must be greater than the height of his body.

- The head is in proportion to the body.

- The ears are low-set.

- The tail is set on high and is carried over the back.

- The nose is black.

In chocolate coloured dogs, the nose may be liver-coloured, and although this looks attractive it makes the dog ineligible for the show ring.

Dentition is hard to judge at this stage, and it may changes as the adult teeth come through. The requirement is for full dentition, which means a total of 42 teeth in the adult dog, 20 in the upper jaw and 22 in the lower jaw.

Historically missing incisors have been a problem, and responsible breeders are striving to improve this aspect of the breed.

There are no certainties when it comes to assessing show potential.

A Lhasa-friendly home

It may seem an age before your Lhasa puppy is ready to leave the breeder and move to his new home. But you can fill the time by getting your home ready, and buying the equipment you will need.

These preparations apply to a new puppy but, in reality, they are the means of creating an environment that is safe and secure for your Lhasa Apso throughout his life.

In the home

Nothing is safe when a puppy is about, and that is certainly true if you have a Lhasa in the house! Everything is new and exciting for a young puppy,

and he will investigate everything with his mouth, which can lead him into all sorts of mischief.

One thing is certain; a free-ranging Lhasa puppy cannot be trusted. Remember, it is not only your prized possessions that are under threat – the damage a puppy can inflict on himself is equally relevant. Trailing electric cables are a major hazard so these will need to be secured out of reach.

You will need to make sure all cupboards and storage units cannot be opened or broken into. This applies particularly in the kitchen where you may store cleaning materials, and other substances, which could be toxic to dogs.

There are a number of household plants that are poisonous, so these will need to be relocated, along with breakable ornaments.

You may decide to declare upstairs off-limits and this is a sensible decision, particularly as negotiating stairs can be hazardous for a young puppy.

The best way of doing this is to install a baby gate; these can also be useful if you want to limit your Lhasa's freedom in any other part of the house.

This barrier works well as your dog is separate but does not feel excluded from what is going on.

In the garden

The Lhasa Apso is a people dog so escaping from his home is rarely on his agenda. He is unlikely to scale the fence or tunnel his way out – but never say never. The sensible dog owner should ensure the garden is fenced to a minimum height of 1m (4 ft) and it should be kept in good repair. If you have gates leading out of your property, they must have secure fastenings. If you are a keen gardener, you may want to think about creating an area of garden that is free from plants and shrubs. A Lhasa may share your passion for gardening but you are unlikely to appreciate his endeavours. Digging holes and uprooting plants is his idea of helping.

If you allow your Lhasa Apso free access to the garden you should be aware that there are a number of plants that are toxic to dogs, such as tulip bulbs, lily of the valley, azaleas, jasmine and daffodil flowers. You can find a comprehensive list on the Internet. You also need to be aware that garden chemicals, such as fertilisers, fungicides and pesticides, are highly toxic so be very careful where you use them. Swimming pools and ponds should be covered, as most puppies are fearless and, although it is easy for a puppy to take the plunge, it is virtually impossible for him to get out, potentially with lethal consequences. You will also need to designate a toileting area. This will assist the house training process, and it will also make cleaning up easier.

House rules

Before your puppy comes home, hold a family conference to make the house rules. You need to decide which rooms your puppy will have access to, and establish whether he is to be allowed on the furniture or not. It is important to start as you mean to go on. You cannot invite a puppy on to the sofa for cuddles only to decide in a few months' time that this is no longer desirable. The Lhasa is a born companion but he can have a stubborn streak. If house rules are applied consistently, he will understand what is, and what is not, allowed, and he will learn to respect you and co-operate with you.

Buying equipment

There are some essential items of equipment you will need for your Lhasa Apso. If you choose wisely, much of it will last for many years to come.

Indoor crate

Rearing a puppy is so much easier if you invest in an indoor crate. It provides a safe haven for your puppy at night, when you have to go out during the day, and at other times when you cannot supervise him.

A puppy needs a base where he feels safe and secure, and where he can rest undisturbed. An indoor crate provides the perfect den, and many adults continue to use them throughout their lives.The crate needs to be big enough for an adult to be able to stand up, turn around, and stretch out in comfort. This means a minimum size of 20 x 15 x 21in high (60x45x52cm).

You will also need to consider where you are going to locate the crate. The kitchen is usually the most suitable place as this is the hub of family life. Try to find a snug corner where the puppy can see what is going on around him, and still be with the family.

Your puppy will need a place where he can rest undisturbed.

Playpen

This is a popular option with many Lhasa owners. A playpen gives your puppy a space where he can move around, play with his toys, watch what is going on, and rest when he is tired – all while being safely confined. You can also move the playpen from one room to another, which means your Lhasa can be with you when you are getting on with other jobs and cannot give him 100 per cent attention.

Beds and bedding

The crate and playpen will need to be lined with bedding and the best type to buy is synthetic fleece. This is warm and cosy and, as moisture soaks through it, your puppy will not have a wet bed when he is tiny and is still unable to go through the night without relieving himself. This type of bedding is machine washable and easy to dry; buy two pieces, so you have one to use while the other piece is in the wash. If you have purchased a crate, you may not feel the need to buy an extra bed, although your Lhasa may like to have his own space in the family room so he feels part of household activities. There is an amazing array of dog-beds to chose from – duvets, bean bags, cushions, baskets, igloos, mini-four posters – so you can take your pick! However, you do need to bear in mind that a puppy may enjoy chewing his bed, so it is probably worth delaying this purchase until your Lhasa has finished teething.

Collar and lead

You may think that it is not worth buying a collar for the first few weeks, but the sooner your pup gets used to it, the better. A nylon lightweight collar is recommended, as most puppies will accept it without making a fuss. Be careful when you are fitting the collar that is not too tight, but equally not too loose as slipping the collar can become a favourite game... A matching webbing lead is a good option as long as it is reasonably lightweight. The most important consideration is that the lead has a secure trigger fastening. An extending lead can be a useful purchase as you can give your Lhasa limited freedom when it is not safe or permitted to allow him off lead. However, you should never use it when walking alongside roads as an unexpected pull from your Lhasa, resulting in the lead extending further than you want, could have disastrous consequences.

ID

Your Lhasa needs to wear some form of ID when he is out in public places. This can be in the form of a disc, engraved with your contact details, attached to the collar. When your Lhasa is full-grown, you can buy an embroidered collar with your contact details, which eliminates the danger of the disc becoming detached from the collar. Microchipping, which is a permanent form of ID, is now a legal requirement in the UK, and increasingly breeders are getting puppies' microchipped before they go to their new homes.

A microchip is the size of a grain of rice. It is injected under the skin, usually between the shoulder blades, with a special needle. It has tiny barbs on it, which dig into the tissue around where it lies, so it does not migrate from that spot. Each chip has its own unique identification number which can only be read by a special scanner. That ID number is then registered on a national database with your name and details, so that if ever your dog is lost, he can be taken to any vet or rescue centre where he is scanned and then you are contacted. If your puppy has not been microchipped, you can ask your vet to do it, maybe when he goes for his vaccinations.

Bowls

Your Lhasa will need two bowls; one for food, and one for fresh drinking water, which should always be readily available. A stainless steel bowl is a good choice for food as it is tough and hygienic. Plastic bowls will almost certainly be chewed, and there is a danger that bacteria can collect in the small cracks

Hold back from buying an expensive bed until your Lhasa has gone through the chewing phase.

that may appear. You can opt for a second stainless steel bowl for drinking water, or you may prefer a heavier ceramic bowl which will not be knocked over so easily.

Food

The breeder will let you know what your puppy is eating and should provide a full diet sheet to guide you through the first six months of your puppy's feeding regime – how much they are eating per meal, how many meals per day, when to increase the amounts given per meal and when to reduce the meals per day. The breeder may provide you with some food when you go and collect your puppy, but it is worth making enquiries in advance about the availability of the brand that is recommended.

Grooming gear

Taking on a long-coated breed means that you will need a full set of grooming equipment. To begin with you will need:

- A good-quality bristle brush

- A steel-toothed comb

- Nail-clippers – the guillotine type are easy to use.

- Toothbrush and toothpaste: choose between a long-handled toothbrush or a finger brush

– whichever you find easiest to use. There are flavoured canine toothpastes on the market which are acceptable to your dog.

The grooming equipment you will need thereafter depends on whether you are keeping your Lhasa in full coat or opting for a pet trim. For more information, see Caring for your Lhasa Apso.

Toys

Lhasa puppies love to play, and there is no shortage of dog toys on the market. But before you get carried away with buying a vast range of toys to keep your puppy entertained, think about possible hazards. A puppy can easily chew bits from soft or plastic toys, and if this material is ingested it can cause serious problems in the form of a blockage.

This is particularly true of toys with squeakers. The safest toys to choose are tug training toys which are made from a variety of materials including rabbit, rope and faux fur. A rubber kong, which can be stuffed with food is a useful purchase as it provides occupation for your Lhasa when you have to leave him home alone. Be careful with the toys you provide when your Lhasa is teething, which is generally around four months of age. His mouth will be sensitive at this time, and tug games could affect the adult teeth as they come through.

Finding a vet

Before your puppy arrives home, you should register with a vet. Visit several vets in your local area, or speak to other pet owners that you might know, to see who they recommend. It is so important to find a good vet – almost as much as finding a good doctor for yourself.

You need to find someone with whom you can build up a good rapport and have complete faith in. Word of mouth is really the best recommendation. When you contact a veterinary practice, find out the following:

- Does the surgery run an appointment system?

- What are the arrangements for emergency, out of hours cover?

- Do any of the vets in the practice have experience treating Lhasa Apsos?

- What facilities are available at the practice?

If you are satisfied with what you find, and the staff appear to be helpful and friendly, book an appointment so your puppy can have a health check a couple of days after you collect him.

Facing page: Check out the veterinary practice before making your first appointment.

Settling in

When you first arrive home with your puppy, be careful not to overwhelm him. You and your family are hugely excited, but the puppy is in a completely strange environment with new sounds, smells and sights, which is a daunting experience, even for the boldest of pups.

Some puppies are very confident, wanting to play straightaway and quickly making friends; others need a little longer. Keep a close check on your puppy's body language and reactions so you can proceed at a pace he is comfortable with.

First, let him explore the garden. He will probably need to relieve himself after the journey home, so take him to the allocated toileting area and, when he performs, give him plenty of praise. When you take your puppy indoors, let him investigate again. Show him his crate, and encourage him to go in by throwing in a treat.

Let him have a sniff, and allow him to go in and out

as he wants to. Later on, when he is tired, you can put him in the crate while you stay in the room. In this way he will learn to settle and will not think he is being abandoned.

It is a good idea to feed your puppy in his crate, at least to begin with, as this helps to build up a positive association. It will not be long before your Lhasa sees his crate as his own special den and will go there as a matter of choice. Some owners place a blanket over the crate, covering the back and sides, so that it is even more cosy and den-like.

Meeting the family

Resist the temptation of inviting friends and neighbours to come and meet the new arrival; your puppy needs to focus on getting to know his new family for the first few days. Try not to swamp your Lhasa with too much attention – he needs a chance to explore and find his feet. There will be plenty of time for cuddles later on!

If you have children in the family, you need to keep everything as calm as possible. The Lhasa will make an outstanding family companion but a sense of mutual respect needs to be established.

As already highlighted, a Yorkie is not the best choice for small children but older children also need to learn how to behave with the new addition to the family.

The Lhasa Apso is small, but he is not a toy, and he is definitely not a baby! He needs to be treated like a proper dog, which means:

- He should not be constantly picked up and carried around.

- He should not be teased.

- He should be left in peace when he retires to his bed.

- He should not be disturbed when he is eating.

Bear in mind, it is easy for a puppy to become over-excited by raised voices, or by children running around and behaving unpredictably, and this can easily lead to mouthing and nipping.

The best plan is to get the children to sit on the floor and give them each a treat. Each child can then call the puppy, stroke him, and offer a treat. In this way the puppy realises that it is not a free for all, and that he needs to interact with each child calmly and sensibly in order to get his treat.

If he tries to nip or mouth, make sure there is a toy at the ready, so his attention can be diverted to something he is allowed to bite.

If you do this consistently, he will learn to inhibit his desire to mouth when he is interacting with people.

Right from the start, impose a rule that the children are not allowed to pick up or carry the puppy. They can cuddle him when they are sitting on the floor. This may sound a little severe, but a wriggly puppy can be dropped in an instant, sometimes with disastrous consequences.

Involve all family members with your puppy's day-to-day care; this will enable the bond to develop with the whole family as opposed to just one person. Encourage the children to train and reward the puppy, teaching him to follow their commands without question.

The animal family

Care must be taken when introducing a puppy to a resident dog to ensure that relations get off on the right footing. Lhasa Apsos are sociable dogs and you will rarely have problems, but it is better to be safe rather than sorry.

Your adult dog may be allowed to meet the puppy at the breeder's, which is ideal as the older dog will not feel threatened if he is away from home. But if this is not possible, allow your dog to smell the puppy's bedding (the bedding supplied by the breeder is fine) before they actually meet so he familiarises himself with the puppy's scent.

The garden is the best place for introducing the puppy, as the adult will regard it as neutral territory. He will probably take a great interest in the puppy and sniff him all over.

Most puppies are naturally submissive in this situation, and your pup may lick the other dog's mouth or roll over on to his back. Try not to interfere as this is the natural way that dogs get to know each other.

You will only need to intervene if the older dog is too boisterous, and alarms the puppy. In this case, it is a good idea to put the adult on his lead so you have some measure of control.

The Lhasa is a confident dog who will get on with other dogs – big or small.

It rarely takes long for an adult to accept a puppy, as he does not constitute a threat. This will be underlined if you make a big fuss of the older dog so that he has no reason to feel jealous. But no matter how well the two dogs are getting on, do not leave them alone unless one is crated.

Feline friends

The Lhasa Apso does not have a strong prey drive but you still need to supervise interactions with a cat in the early stages. It is best to progress step by step, making sure that your puppy and cat are never left alone together until they have learnt to ignore each other.

If your Lhasa seems very focused on the cat, it may be easier to confine him in a carrier for the first couple of meetings so your puppy has a chance to make his acquaintance in a controlled situation. Keep calling your puppy to you and rewarding him so that he does not get obsessed with cat watching.

You can then graduate to holding your puppy while the cat is free, again rewarding him with a treat every time he responds to you and looks away from the cat. When you allow your puppy to go free, make sure the cat has an easy escape route, just in case he tries to chase.This is an on-going process but all the time your Lhasa is learning that he is rewarded for ignoring the cat. In time, the novelty will wear off and the pair will live in peace – who knows, they may even become the best of friends?

Feeding

The breeder will generally provide enough food for the first few days so the puppy does not have to cope with a change in diet – and possible digestive upset – along with all the stress of moving home.

Some puppies eat up their food from the first meal onwards, others are more concerned by their new surroundings and are too distracted to eat. If your puppy seems disinterested in his food, give him 10 minutes to eat what he wants and then remove the leftovers and start afresh at the next meal. Obviously if you have any concerns about your puppy in the first few days, seek advice from your vet. It is important to give your dog space where he can eat in peace, and if you have children, you need to establish a rule that no one is to go near the dog when he is feeding.

The first night

Your puppy will have spent the first weeks of his life with either his mother or curled up with his siblings. He is then taken from everything he knows as familiar, lavished with attention by his new family, and then comes bed time when he is left all alone. It is little wonder that he feels abandoned.

The best plan is to establish a night-time routine, and then stick to it so that your puppy knows what is expected of him. Take your puppy out into the garden to relieve himself, and then settle him in his crate. Some people leave a low light on for the puppy at night for the first week, others have tried a radio as company or a ticking clock. A covered hot-water bottle, filled with warm water, can also be a comfort. Like people, puppies are all individuals and what works for one, does not necessarily work for another, so it is a matter of trial and error.

Be very positive when you leave your puppy on his own; do not linger, or keep returning; this will make the situation more difficult. It is inevitable that he will protest to begin with, but if you stick to your routine, he will accept that he gets left at night but you always return in the morning.

Coping alone

Following on from establishing a night-time routine, it is important that your Lhasa learns to be left for periods of time during the day. As already highlighted, the Lhasa does not relish time without his special people but he needs to understand that if he is left home alone, there is no cause for anxiety.

Facing page: It is inevitable that your puppy will miss his littermates for the first few nights.

Work on the following regime so your puppy is relaxed about the family's comings and goings:

- Settle your puppy in his crate, making sure he has toileted.

- Provide a kong, filled with food, so he has something to do while you are absent.

- Keep your leave-taking preparations to a minimum (so your puppy does not start to anticipate, and dread, your departure).

- Do not make a big thing out of saying goodbye. Leave your puppy calmly and quietly.

When you return, do not rush to the crate to release him, giving him a huge greeting. Leave it a few minutes and then approach his crate, talking to him quietly, before letting him out.

To begin with, try to keep your absences fairly short – about an hour's duration – and gradually build up the time you are away as your puppy learns to settle.

Rescued dogs

Settling an older, rescued dog in the home is very similar to a puppy in as much as you will need to make the same preparations regarding his homecoming.

As with a puppy, an older dog will need you to be

consistent, so start as you mean to go on. There is often an initial honeymoon period when you bring a rescued dog home, where he will be on his best behaviour for the first few weeks. It is after these first couple of weeks that the true nature of the dog will show, so be prepared for subtle changes in his behaviour. It may be advisable to register with a reputable training club, so you can seek advice on any training or behavioural issues at an early stage.

Above all, remember that a rescued dog ceases to be a rescued dog the moment he enters his forever home and should be treated normally like any other family pet.

A rescued dog will need your patience and understanding as he settles in his new home.

House training

This is an aspect of training that first-time owners dread, but if you start as you mean to go on, it will not be long before your Lhasa Apso understands what is required.

The key to successful house training is vigilance and consistency. If you establish a routine, and you stick to it, your puppy will understand what is required.

Equally, you must be there to supervise him at all times, except when he is safely tucked up in his crate. It is when a puppy is left to wander from room to room that accidents are most likely to happen.

As discussed earlier, you will have allocated a toileting area in your garden when preparing for your puppy's homecoming. You need to take your puppy to this area every time he needs to relieve himself so he builds up an association and knows why you have

brought him out to the garden.

Establish a routine and make sure you take your puppy out at the following times:

- First thing in the morning
- After mealtimes
- On waking from a sleep
- Following a play session
- Last thing at night.

A puppy should be taken out to relieve himself every two hours as an absolute minimum. If you can manage an hourly trip out, so much the better.

The more often your puppy gets it right, the quicker he will learn to be clean in the house. It helps if you use a verbal cue, such as 'Busy', when your pup is performing and, in time, this will trigger the desired response.

Do not be tempted to put your puppy out on the doorstep in the hope that he will toilet on his own. Most pups simply sit there, waiting to get back inside the house! No matter how bad the weather is, accompany your puppy and give him lots of praise when he performs correctly.

Do not rush back inside as soon as he has finished;

your puppy might start to delay in the hope of prolonging his time outside with you. Praise him, have a quick game, and then you can both return indoors.

When accidents happen

No matter how vigilant you are, there are bound to be accidents. If you witness the accident, take your puppy outside immediately, and give him lots of praise if he finishes his business out there.

If you are not there when he has an accident, do not scold him when you discover what has happened. He will not remember what he has done and will not understand why you are cross with him. Simply clean it up and resolve to be more vigilant next time.

Make sure you use a deodoriser, available in pet stores, when you clean up otherwise your pup will be drawn to the smell and may be tempted to use the same spot again.

Choosing a diet

There are so many different types of dog food on sale, all claiming to be the best, so how do you know what is likely to suit your Lhasa Apso?

When choosing a diet, there are basically three categories to choose from:

Complete

This is probably the most popular diet as it is easy to feed and is specially formulated with all the nutrients your dog needs. This means that you should not add any supplements or you may upset the nutritional balance. Most complete diets come in different life stages: puppy, adult maintenance and senior, so this means that your Lhasa is getting what he needs when he is growing, during adulthood, and as he becomes older. You can even get prescription diets for dogs with particular health issues.

Check protein levels provided in the diet; it is important that your Lhasa has the correct level depending on his age and lifestyle. Puppies and juniors need 25-35 per cent of protein in the diet for growth and development; 18-20 per cent protein is adequate for adult maintenance and veterans needs a much lower level, decreasing from the basic adult maintenance diet.

There are many different brands to choose from so it is advisable to seek advice from your puppy's breeder who will have lengthy experience of feeding Lhasa Apsos.

Canned/ pouches

This type of food is usually fed with hard biscuit, and most Lhasas find it very appetising. However, the ingredients and the nutritional value do vary significantly between the different brands so you will need to check the label. This type of food often has a high moisture content, so you need to be sure your Lhasa is getting all the nutrition he needs.

Homemade

There are some owners who like to prepare meals especially for their dogs – and it is probably much appreciated. The danger is that although the food is tasty, and your Lhasa may appreciate the variety, you cannot be sure that it has the correct nutritional balance.

If this is a route you want to go down, you will need to find out the exact ratio of fats, carbohydrates, proteins, minerals and vitamins that are needed, which is quite an undertaking.

The Barf (Biologically Appropriate Raw Food) diet is another, more natural approach to feeding. Dogs are fed a diet mimicking what they would have eaten in the wild, consisting of raw meat, bone, muscle, fat, and vegetable matter. There are now a number of companies that specialise in producing the Barf diet in frozen form, which makes it easy for a small dog to eat – and you do not have to get involved in time consuming preparation.

Feeding regime

When your puppy arrives in his new home he will need four meals, evenly spaced throughout the day. You may decide to keep to the diet recommended by your puppy's breeder, and if your pup is thriving there is no need to change. However, if your puppy is not doing well on the food, or you have problems with supply, you will need to make a change.

When switching diets, it is very important to do it on a gradual basis, changing over from one food to the next, a little at a time, and spreading the transition over a week to 10 days. This will avoid the risk of digestive upset.

From about 12 weeks, you can go down to three meals a day, and by six months, you can feed twice daily – a regime which should suit your Lhasa for the rest of his life.

Faddy feeders

Some Lhasa Apsos are very keen on their food, others are less enthusiastic and this can lead to problems, especially if you have a single dog who can leave food without risk of losing it.

Do not over-indulge your Lhasa Apso as this may cause him to become fussy in his feeding habits.

If your Lhasa starts leaving his food, you should observe him closely in case this is a sign that he is unwell. If you fear this is the case, you will need to consult your vet. However, it could be that he is bored with his food and is holding out for something better. One look from those bewitching eyes is enough to melt your heart, stirring you to greater efforts in the hope of finding a food that your Lhasa really likes. At first you may add some gravy, then you may try some chicken... A clever Lhasa will quickly realise that if he holds out, tastier treats will follow.This is a bad game to play as not only will you run out of tempting delicacies, you will also be losing your Lhasa's respect.

If your Lhasa is turning up his nose at mealtimes, give him 10 minutes to eat what he wants, and then take up his bowl. Do not feed him treats in between meals, and give him fresh food at his next mealtime. If you continue this regime for a couple of days, your Lhasa will realise that there is no percentage in holding out for better food as it never materialises.

In most cases, this is just a 'trying it on' phase, and if you cope with common sense, you will soon return to the status quo and your Lhasa will be content with his normal rations.

If, however, your dog refuses all food for more than 24 hours you need to observe his behaviour to see if there are any signs of ill health, which may involve the need for a veterinary check up.

Bones and chews

Puppies love to chew, and many adults also enjoy gnawing on a bone. A raw marrow bone is ideal, but make sure it is always given under supervision.

White, sterilised bones do not make as much mess as a raw marrow bone, and they have the same end result of helping to keep your dog's teeth clean.

Rawhide chews are best avoided; it is all too easy for a Lhasa to bite off a chunk and swallow it, with the danger of it then causing a blockage.

Your Lhasa will appreciate the occasional bone or chew.

Ideal weight

In order to help to keep your Lhasa Apso in good health it is necessary to monitor his weight. If your dog gets sufficient exercise and is fed a diet that matches his energy output, he should not put on weight. But it is something you should monitor closely.

A dog that is carrying too much weight is vulnerable to many health issues; he has a reduced quality of life as he cannot exercise properly, and he will almost certainly have a reduced life expectancy.

If your Lhasa has a pet trim you will be able to see his body shape. Look at him from above, and make sure you can see a definite waist. You should be able to feel his ribs, but not see them.

If your Lhasa is in full coat, establish what is the optimum weight for his size and then get into the habit of weighing him on a regular basis so you can keep a check on him.

If you are worried that your Lhasa is putting on too much weight, or equally if you think he is underweight, consult your vet who will help you to plan a suitable diet.

Facing page: A lean active dog will enjoy a better quality of life.

Caring for your Lhasa Apso

The Lhasa Apso is a relatively easy dog to care for in terms of feeding and exercise – but his coat is another matter. However, you would not have taken on a Lhasa unless you enjoyed grooming...

During the course of his life, a Lhasa Apso will spend a fair proportion of his time being groomed so it is important to make this experience as pleasurable as possible. If your Lhasa learns to relax and enjoys the quality time he is spending with you, it will enrich your relationship with each other.

Puppy care

A Lhasa puppy has a short dense coat, which needs regular brushing and combing. However, he is going to need much more attention as his coat grows so it is important that he becomes used to the whole

grooming process. Even if you opt for a pet/puppy trim, your Lhasa will need regular trips to the groomer, and so he needs to be relaxed about being handled.

In addition, a grooming session gives you the opportunity to check your dog and to discover any minor problems, such as sore places, or any abnormalities, such as lumps and bumps, which may need to be investigated. Remember, if you spot a problem early on, you increase the chance of an early diagnosis and successful treatment.

The first step is to get your puppy used to being handled so that he accepts the attention without resentment. The best plan is to place a rubber mat on a table so your puppy feels secure and you are at the right height to groom him. Initially, he will wriggle and attempt to mouth you, but just ignore his protests.

Hold him steady for a few moments, and reward him when he is still. A puppy needs to learn that it is OK to be touched all over; if you fail to do this, he may try to warn you off by growling, which could develop into more problematic behaviour.

Start by handling your puppy all over, stroking him from his head to his tail. Lift up each paw in turn, and reward him with a treat when he co-operates.

Then roll him over on to his back and tickle his tummy; this is a very vulnerable position for a dog to adopt, so do not force the issue. Be firm but gentle, and give your Lhasa Apso lots of praise when he does as you ask.

When your Lhasa is happy to be handled in this way, you can introduce a bristle brush and spend a few minutes working on his coat, and then rewarding him.

Follow this up by working through the coat with a steel-toothed comb. Your puppy will gradually learn to accept the attention, and will relax while you groom him.

Bathing

The Lhasa Apso needs frequent bathing, twice weekly for pet dogs and weekly for show dogs. Again, you will reap the benefits if your puppy gets used to being bathed when he is a puppy.

Selecting the correct shampoo and conditioner is essential for a full-coated Lhasa; it is a good idea to seek guidance from an experienced exhibitor. This is not so crucial with a Lhasa in pet trim but it is best to opt for good-quality products.

With pet trims and full coats, the coat needs to be thoroughly groomed before bathing to make sure there are no mats or tangles – these will be impossible to get rid of once the coat is wet.

The Lhasa is small enough to be bathed in a sink, or you may prefer to use the bath or a shower cubicle. In all instances, use a rubber mat to create a non-slippery surface for your Lhasa to stand on. Then proceed as follows:

- Wet the coat thoroughly, using luke-warm water, and then apply the shampoo.

- Work the shampoo into a rich lather and then rinse, making sure you get rid of all traces of shampoo. A full-coated Lhasa may need to be shampooed twice to ensure he is clean right down to the skin.

- Apply the conditioner, diluted in a jug and leave it on for 3-5 minutes. Then rinse again.

- Squeeze out the excess water from the coat, and then use a towel to absorb as much moisture as possible. If your Lhasa is full-coated, take care not to rub the coat, as this will cause it to tangle.

- Use a hair-dryer, on a moderate setting to dry the coat. If your dog has a full coat, make sure you direct the dryer to one area of the coat at a time and brush as you dry.

Pet trim

If you have no plans to exhibit your Lhasa Apso in the show ring, you will probably opt to keep him in a pet trim, also known as a 'puppy' or 'teddy' trim. There are minor variations but this entails:

A pet trim is a sensible option if you have no plans to show exhibit your dog in the show ring.

- A short body coat.

- Furnishings on the head are trimmed so the eyes are visible, and the beard is short.

- The front legs and hindquarters are trimmed to give a trouser effect.

- The hair on the tail is trimmed but with sufficient length so it falls in a plume over the back.

To maintain a pet trim you will need to take your Lhasa to a professional groomer every six to eight weeks – unless you have the skill to tackle the job yourself.

In-between trims, you will need to groom every day using a soft slicker brush, and then comb through the longer hair to prevent mats and tangles forming. There is still a reasonable amount of work involved to ensure your Lhasa is clean and tidy – but this is nothing in comparison to caring for a full-coated Lhasa.

Full coat

Caring for a Lhasa Apso in full coat is a tremendous undertaking as you are working on the twin goals of allowing your dog sufficient freedom to exercise freely and to be a dog, while at the same time trying to preserve his magnificent coat in its full splendour.

Most Lhasa owners find their own way of protecting the coat, outside show times, by tying or plaiting the head furnishings, and banding the hair around the hindquarters.

You can also use a coat to keep the body hair out of the mud and rain! However, Lhasa exhibitors accept that weekly bathing and lengthy daily grooming is a must.

Traditionally the hair is parted along the length of the back; a pin brush is best for this job. The coat can then be brushed through using a bristle/nylon mix brush. A comb can be used to gently tease out tangles; it will help if you use a spray on conditioner as this ensures you do not damage the hair. In terms of trimming, the Lhasa should not look highly coiffured but the head-fall may need to be trimmed, and you may also need to do some general tidying up to give your Lhasa the balanced appearance that is required. Trimming should be scheduled two or three weeks in advance of the show to give the coat a chance to settle.

Routine care

In addition to grooming, you will need to carry out some routine care.

Eyes

Check the eyes for signs of soreness or discharge. You can use a piece of cotton wool (cotton) – a separate piece for each eye – and wipe away any debris.

Ears

The ears should be clean and free from odour. You can buy specially manufactured ear wipes, or you can use a piece of cotton wool to clean them if necessary. Do not probe into the ear canal or you risk doing more harm than good. You will also need to pluck out excess hair from the ear canal.

Teeth

Dental disease is becoming more prevalent among dogs, and this is particularly the case with small breeds. Teeth cleaning should therefore be seen as an essential part of your care regime. The build up of tartar on the teeth can result in tooth decay, gum infection and bad breath, and if it is allowed to accumulate, you may have no option but to get the teeth cleaned under anaesthetic. When your Lhasa is still a puppy, accustom him to teeth cleaning so it becomes a matter of routine. Dog toothpaste comes in a variety of meaty flavours, which your Lhasa will like, so you can start by putting some toothpaste on your finger and gently rubbing his teeth. You can then progress to using a finger brush or a toothbrush, whichever you find most convenient. Remember to reward your Lhasa when he co-operates and then he will positively look forward to his teeth-cleaning sessions.

Nails

Nail trimming is a task dreaded by many owners, and many dogs, but if you start early on, your Lhasa will get used to the task you have to perform and will not fight against it. Depending on coat colour, nails may be black or white. If the nail is white, you will be able to

It is important that your Lhasa feels relaxed when he is on the grooming table.

The ears should be clean and free from odour.

Regular teeth cleaning should be considered essential.

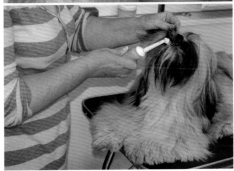

see the quick (the vein that runs through the nail), which you must avoid at all costs. If you cut the quick it will bleed profusely and cause considerable discomfort. In black and dark-coloured nails, the quick is not visible so the best policy is to trim little and often. Then the nails don't grow too long, and you do not risk cutting too much and catching the quick. If you are worried about trimming your Lhasa Apso's nails, go to your veterinary practice and a nurse will show you what to do. If you are still concerned, you can always use the services of a professional groomer.

Rear end

Check your Lhasa's rear end to ensure the hair is not soiled when he has toiletted, which is a problem with long-coated breeds. Even if your Lhasa has a pet trim you will need to keep a regular check on his personal hygiene; it will help if the groomer trims the hair around the anus, which will make your job easier. Many pet owners give their dogs a 'bath and bottom trim' in-between trips to the groomer.

Exercise

The Lhasa Apso is a busy, active dog and he should be given the opportunity to run and play. He is an inquisitive dog and will relish the chance to go to new places and investigate the sights and smells.

Facing page: Your Lhasa will enjoy going out and about – whatever the weather...

For the first six months, your Lhasa will get as much exercise as he needs playing in the garden, in addition to taking him out to socialise him (see Social Skills). Lead walking should be carefully monitored as walking on a hard surface is more tiring than you think, and you do not want your puppy to be exhausted either mentally or physically.

The Lhasa is an adaptable little dog and as he matures he will be capable of more strenuous exercise but, equally, he will be content with shorter outings. Obviously you want to keep your dog fit, but it is equally important to provide mental stimulation.

This means including him in the comings and goings of family life, and spending time interacting him. This could include playing games, teaching tricks, training or grooming him – it doesn't matter what you do, as long as your spending quality time with your dog.

The older Lhasa

We are fortunate that the Lhasa Apso has a good life expectancy – generally around 12-14 years, and some may do even better. As your Lhasa grows older, he may sleep more and he may be reluctant to go for longer walks. He may show signs of stiffness when he gets up from his bed, but these generally ease when he starts moving.

Some older Lhasas may have impaired vision, and some may become a little deaf, but as long as their senses do not deteriorate dramatically, this is something older dogs learn to live with.

If you treat your older dog with kindness and consideration, he will enjoy his later years and suffer the minimum of discomfort. It is advisable to switch him over to a senior diet, which is more suited to his needs, and you may need to adjust the quantity, as he will not be burning up the calories as he did when he was younger and more energetic.

The older Lhasa will prefer a softer diet, and you will need to keep a close check on his teeth as these may cause problems. Make sure his sleeping quarters are warm and free from draughts, and if he gets wet, make sure you dry him thoroughly.

Most important of all, be guided by your Lhasa Apso. He will have good days when he feels up to going for a walk, and other days when he would prefer to potter in the garden.

If you have a younger dog at home, this may well stimulate your Lhasa to take more of an interest in what is going on, but make sure he is not pestered as he needs to rest undisturbed when he is tired.

Letting go

Inevitably there comes a time when your Lhasa is not enjoying a good quality of life, and you need to make the painful decision to let him go. We would all wish that our dogs died, painlessly, in their sleep but, unfortunately, this is rarely the case.

However, we can allow our dogs to die with dignity, and to suffer as little as possible, and this should be our way of saying thank you for the wonderful companionship they have given us.

When you feel the time is drawing close, talk to your vet who will be able to make an objective assessment of your Lhasa's condition and will help you to make the right decision.

This is the hardest thing you will ever have to do as a dog owner, and it is only natural to grieve for your beloved Lhasa. But eventually you will be able to look back on the happy memories of times spent together, and this will bring much comfort.

You may, in time, feel that your life is not complete without a Lhasa Apso and you will feel ready to welcome a new puppy into your home.

Facing page: In time, you may feel ready to welcome another Lhasa Apso into your home.

Social skills

To live in the modern world, without fears and anxieties, your Lhasa Apso needs to receive an education in social skills so that he learns to cope calmly and confidently in a wide variety of situations. The Lhasa is a self-assured dog, with few hang-ups, and will relish the opportunity to broaden his horizons.

Early learning

The breeder will have begun a programme of socialisation by getting the puppies used to all the sights and sounds of a busy household.

You need to continue this when your pup arrives in his new home, making sure he is not worried by household equipment, such as the vacuum cleaner or the washing machine, and that he gets used to unexpected noises from the radio and television.

To begin with, your puppy needs to get used to all the members of his new family, but then you should give him the opportunity to meet friends and other people who visit your home.

If you do not have children, make sure your puppy has the chance to meet and play with other people's children, making sure interactions are always supervised, so he learns that people come in small sizes too.

The Lhasa Apso loves his family but he can be wary of strangers. A warning bark is acceptable when a visitor comes to your house but then you want your Lhasa to take the lead from you and welcome the visitor into your home.

To teach your Lhasa to accept the comings and goings of a busy household, follow these guidelines.

You will need to recruit a friend to help you with your training programme.

- Arrange for a friend to come to your house and when they are at the door, attach a lead to your Lhasa and make sure you have some treats at the ready.

- When you open the door, distract your Lhasa by giving him some treats.

- Then ask your friend to give him some treats.

- When your Lhasa is showing relaxed body language, invite your friend into the house.

- Go into the kitchen/sitting room and sit down for a few minutes, still keeping your dog on the lead. Do not pay too much attention to your Lhasa, let him take in the situation so that he realises there is no need to react.

- When he is settled, let him off the lead, first making sure your friend has some treats. If your Lhasa approaches your friend he can be rewarded with treats and then he should be ignored.

Practise this scenario on a few occasions so that your Lhasa learns meeting and greeting manners and does not feel that visitors pose a threat.

The outside world

When your puppy has completed his vaccinations, he is ready to venture into the outside world. Lhasa Apsos are generally pretty confident but there is a lot for a youngster to take on board, so do not swamp him with too many new experiences when you first set out.

Obviously you need to work at lead training before you go on your first expedition. There will be plenty of distractions to cope with, so you do not want additional problems of coping with a dog that is pulling or lagging on the lead.

Hopefully, you can set off with your Lhasa walking by your side on a loose lead. He may need additional encouragement when you venture further afield, so arm yourself with some extra special treats, which will give him a good reason to focus on you when required!

Start socialising your puppy in a quiet area with light traffic, and only progress to a busier place when he is ready.

There is so much to see and hear – people (maybe carrying bags or umbrellas), pushchairs, bicycles, cars, lorries, machinery – so give your puppy a chance to take it all in.

If he does appear worried, do not fall into the trap of sympathising with him or over-doing the reassurance.

This will only teach your pup that he had a good reason to be worried and, with luck, you will rescue him if he feels scared.

Instead, give him a little space so he does not have to confront whatever he is frightened of, and distract him with a few treats.

Then encourage him to walk past, using an encouraging tone of voice, never forcing him by yanking on the lead. Reward him for any forward movement, and your puppy will soon learn that he can trust you, and there is nothing to fear.

Your pup also needs to continue his education in canine manners, started by his mother and by his littermates, as he needs to be able to greet all dogs calmly, giving the signals that say he is friendly and offers no threat.

If you have a friend who has a dog of sound temperament, this is an ideal way to get your puppy used to social interactions. As he gets older and more established, you can widen his circle of canine acquaintances.

Training classes

A training class will give your Lhasa Apso the opportunity to work alongside other dogs in a controlled situation, and he will also learn to focus on you in a different, distracting environment. Both these lessons will be vital as your dog matures.

However, the training class needs to be of the highest calibre or you risk doing more harm than good. Before you go along with your puppy, attend a class as an observer to make sure you are happy with what goes on.

• How much training experience do the instructors have?

• Are the classes divided into appropriate age categories?

• Do the instructors have experience training Lhasa Apsos?

• Do they use positive, reward-based training methods?

If the training class is well run, it is certainly worth attending. Both you and your Lhasa Apso will learn useful training exercises; it will increase his social skills, and you will have the chance to talk to lots of like-minded dog enthusiasts.

Facing Page: Positive experience will boost your puppy's confidence.

Training guidelines

The Lhasa Apso is a clever dog and he thrives on mental stimulation. In order to build a successful training partnership, you need to get into the Lhasa mind-set so you understand what makes him tick.

This is a dog that is quick to learn, but he is easily bored. He sees no point in monotonous repetition, and if you become negative in your approach, he will simply switch off. Do not expect instant obedience from your Lhasa; aim for a spirit of co-operation and, hopefully a lot of fun and entertainment along the way.

You will be keen to get started but in your rush to get training underway, do not neglect the fundamentals which could make the difference between success and failure.

When you start training, try to observe the following guidelines:

Choose an area that is free from distractions so your puppy will focus on you. You can move on to a more challenging environment as your pup progresses.

Do not train your puppy just after he has eaten or when you have returned from exercise. He will either be too full, or too tired, to concentrate.

Do not train if you are in a bad mood, or if you are short of time. These sessions always end in disaster!

Providing a worthwhile reward is an essential tool in training. Food is usually the best option for a Lhasa Apso, using high value treats such as cheese, sausage or cooked liver.

Occasionally you will find a Lhasa prefers to be rewarded with a toy. If this is the case, make sure it is only brought out for training sessions so that it accrues added value.

Keep your verbal cues simple, and always use the same one for each exercise. For example, when you ask your puppy to go into the down position, the cue is "down", not "lie down, "get down", or anything else.

Remember, your Lhasa does not speak English; he

associates the sound of the word with the action.

If your dog is finding an exercise difficult, break it down into small steps so it is easier to understand. A Lhasa can dig in his heels so you need to think creatively and give frequent rewards.

Do not make your training sessions boring and repetitious; your Lhasa will lose concentration and will cease to co-operate.

Do not train for too long, particularly with a young puppy, who has a very short attention span, and always end training sessions on a positive note. This does not necessarily mean getting an exercise right. If your pup is tired and making mistakes, ask him to do a simple exercise so you have the opportunity to praise and reward him. You may well find that he benefits from having a break and will make better progress next time you try.

Above all, make training fun so you and your Lhasa enjoy spending quality time together.

First lessons

Like all puppies, a young Lhasa Apso will soak up new experiences like a sponge, so training should start from the time your pup arrives in his new home.

Wearing a collar

You may, or may not, want your Lhasa Apso wear a collar all the time – this may well depend on whether you are keeping him in full coat.

But when he goes out in public places he will need to be on a lead, and so he should be used to the feel of a collar around his neck. The best plan is to accustom your pup to wearing a soft collar for a few minutes at a time until he gets used to it.

Fit the collar so that you can get at least two fingers between the collar and his neck. Then have a game to distract his attention.

This will work for a few moments; then he will stop, put his back leg up behind his neck and scratch away at the peculiar itchy thing which feels so odd.

Bend down, rotate the collar, pat him on the head and distract him by playing with a toy or giving him a treat. Once he has worn the collar for a few minutes each day, he will soon ignore it and become used to it.

Remember, never leave the collar on the puppy unsupervised, especially when he is outside in the garden, or when he is in his crate, as it is could get snagged, causing serious injury.

Walking on the lead

This is a simple exercise but the Lhasa Apso can take exception if you try to rush your training. If you try to force the issue, your Lhasa could throw a tantrum and do everything in his power to escape the restriction or, he may opt for a sit down strike.

All this can be avoided if you progress slowly and reward your Lhasa with tasty treats when he co-operates.

Once your puppy is used to the collar, take him outside into your secure garden where there are no distractions. Attach the lead and, to begin with, allow him to wander with the lead trailing, making sure it does not become snagged on anything.

Then pick up the lead and follow the pup where he wants to go; he needs to get used to the sensation of being attached to you. The next stage is to get your Lhasa to follow you, and for this you will need some treats. To give yourself the best chance of success, make sure the treats are high value (cheese, sausage or cooked liver) so your Lhasa is motivated to work with you.

Show him you have a treat in your hand, and then encourage him to follow you. Walk a few paces, and if he is walking with you, stop and reward him. If he puts on the brakes, simply change direction and lure him with the treat.

Next, introduce some changes of direction so your puppy is walking confidently alongside you. At this stage, introduce a verbal cue – "heel" – when your puppy is in the correct position.

You can then graduate to walking your puppy outside the home, as long as he has completed his vaccination programme, starting in quiet areas and building up to busier environments.

Come when called

The Lhasa Apso wants to be with his people but he is an independent thinker and they may be times when he is distracted. There are so many enticing smells, places to explore, dogs to meet... He will never stray too far away, but he may get into the habit of coming in his own time unless you make the recall a rewarding exercise.

Your aim must be to make coming when called even more rewarding than anything else on your Lhasa Apso's personal agenda.

This needs to be built up over a period of time, with lots of repetition, so your Lhasa sees you as a fun person that is always ready to reward him, rather than as an irate owner who is trying to spoil his fun.

Hopefully, the breeder will have laid the foundations simply by calling the puppies to "come" when it is dinnertime, or when they are moving from one place to another.

You can build on this when your puppy arrives in his new home, calling him to "come" when he is in a confined space, such as the kitchen. This is a good place to build up a positive association with the verbal cue – particularly if you ask your puppy to "come" to get his dinner!

The next stage is to transfer the lesson to the garden. Arm yourself with some treats, and wait until your puppy is distracted. Then call him, using a higher-pitched, excited tone of voice.

At this stage, a puppy wants to be with you, so capitalise on this and keep practising the verbal cue, and rewarding your puppy with a treat and lots of praise when he comes to you.

Now you are ready to introduce some distractions. Try calling him when someone else is in the garden, or wait a few minutes until he is investigating a really interesting scent.

When he responds, make a really big fuss of him and give him extra treats so he knows it is worth his while to come to you.

If he is slow to come, run away a few steps and then call again, making yourself sound really exciting. Jump up and down, open your arms wide to welcome him; it doesn't matter how silly you look, he needs to see you as the most fun person in the world.

When you have a reliable recall in the garden, you can venture into the outside world. Do not be too ambitious to begin with; try a recall in a quiet place with the minimum of distractions so you can be more certain of success.

Do not make the mistake of only asking your dog to come at the end of his allotted exercise period. What is the incentive in coming back to you if all you do is clip on his lead, marking the end of his free time? Instead, call your dog at random times, giving him a treat and a stroke, and then letting him go free again. In this way, coming to you – and focusing on you – is always rewarding.

Stationary exercises

The sit and down are easy to teach, and mastering these exercises will be rewarding for both you and your Lhasa Apso.

Sit

The best method is to lure your Lhasa into position, and for this you can use a treat or his food bowl.

Hold the reward (a treat or food bowl) above his head. As he looks up, he will lower his hindquarters and go into a sit.

Practise this a few times and when your puppy understands what you are asking, introduce the verbal cue, "sit".

When your Lhasa understands the exercise, he will respond to the verbal cue alone, and you will not need to reward him every time he sits.

However, it is a good idea to give him a treat on a random basis when he co-operates to keep him guessing!

Down

This is an important lesson, and can be a lifesaver if an emergency arises and you need to bring your Lhasa Apso to an instant halt.

You can start with your dog in a sit or a stand for this exercise. Stand or kneel in front of him and show him you have a treat in your hand.

Hold the treat just in front of his nose and slowly lower it towards the ground, between his front legs.

As your Lhasa follows the treat he will go down on his front legs and, in a few moments, his hindquarters will follow.

Close your hand over the treat so he doesn't cheat and get the treat before he is in the correct position. As soon as he is in the down, give him the treat and lots of praise.

Keep practising, and when your Lhasa understands what you want, introduce the verbal cue, "down".

When your Lhasa understands the exercise, you can work on increasing duration.

Control exercises

These exercises are not the most exciting, but they are important in establishing a relationship of mutual respect with your Lhasa Apso.

Wait

This exercise teaches your Lhasa to wait in position until you give the next command; it differs from the stay exercise where he must stay where you have left him for a more prolonged period.

The most useful application of wait is when you are getting your dog out of the car and you need him to stay in position until you clip on his lead.

Start with your puppy on the lead to give you a greater chance of success.

Ask him to sit, and stand in front him. Step back one pace, holding your hand, palm flat, facing him.

Wait a second and then come back to stand in front of him. You can then reward him and release him with a word, such as "OK".

Practise this a few times, waiting a little longer before you reward him, and then introduce the verbal cue, "wait".

You can reinforce the lesson by using it in different situations, such as asking your Lhasa to "wait" before you put his food bowl down.

Stay

You need to differentiate this exercise from the wait by putting your Lhasa in the down to start with (he is most likely to be secure in this position) and using a different verbal cue.

Stand by his side and then step forwards, with your hand held back, palm facing the dog.

Step back, release him, and then reward him. Practise until your Lhasa understands the exercise and then introduce the verbal cue, "stay".

Gradually increase the distance you can leave your puppy, and increase the challenge by walking around him – and even stepping over him – so that he learns he must stay until you release him.

Leave

A response to this verbal cue means that your Lhasa Apso will learn to give up a toy on request, and it follows on that he will give up anything when he is asked, which is very useful if he has got hold of a forbidden object. This is very important as the Lhasa has a tendency to become possessive over things he values.

The leave command can be taught quite easily when you are first playing with your puppy. As you gently take a toy from his mouth, introduce the verbal cue, "leave", and then praise him.

If he is reluctant, swap the toy for another toy or a treat. This will usually do the trick.

Do not try to pull the toy from his mouth if he refuses to give it up, as you will make the situation confrontational.

The Lhasa has a stubborn streak and he does not give in easily. The best strategy is to let the toy go dead in your hand, and then swap it for a new toy, or a really high-value treat, so this becomes the better option. Remember to make a big fuss of your Lhasa when he does as you ask. Never stint on giving him verbal praise and telling him he is the best dog in the world!

Opportunities
for Lhasas

The Lhasa Apso is one of the most entertaining of all breeds, and you will certainly have fun if you take on new challenges. The key is to be realistic in your expectations; training provides the opportunity to spend quality time interacting with your Lhasa – it is about taking part, not winning...

Good Citizen Scheme

The Kennel Club Good Citizen Scheme was introduced to promote responsible dog ownership, and to teach dogs basic good manners. In the US there is one test; in the UK there are four award levels: Puppy Foundation, Bronze, Silver and Gold.

Exercises within the scheme include:
- Walking on lead
- Road walking
- Control at door/gate.
- Food manners
- Recall
- Stay
- Send to bed
- Emergency stop.

Obedience

If your Lhasa Apso has mastered basic obedience, you may want to get involved in competitive obedience. The exercises include: heelwork at varying paces with dog and handler following a pattern decided by the judge, stays, recalls, retrieves, sendaways, scent discrimination and distance control. The exercises get progressively harder as you progress up the classes.

Your Lhasa will have no trouble learning these exercise but you need to be aware that this discipline calls for a very high degree of precision and accuracy which does not suit all dogs, or all handlers.

Agility

This is a sport for canine athletes with speed as a prerequisite for success. The Lhasa can compete in the classes for small dogs, and if you get him motivated, he may surprise you with how well he gets on. In Agility, the dog completes an obstacle course, which includes jumps, tunnels, weaving poles and contact equipment (A-frame, dog-walk and seesaw) under the guidance of his owner. You completes the course off the lead. In competition, each dog completes the course individually and is assessed on both time and accuracy. The dog that finishes the course with the fewest faults, in the fastest time, wins the class.

Motivation is key in getting your Lhasa to work for you.

Rally O

If you do not want to get involved in the rigours of Competitive Obedience, you may find that a sport called Rally O is more to your liking. This is loosely based on Obedience, and also has a few exercises borrowed from agility when you get to the highest levels. Handler and dog must complete a course, in the designated order, which has a variety of different exercises which could number from 12 to 20. The course is timed and the team must complete within the time limit that is set, but there are no bonus marks for speed.

The great advantage of Rally O is that it is very relaxed, and anyone can compete; indeed, it has proved very popular for handlers with disabilities as they are able to work their dogs to a high standard and compete on equal terms with other competitors.

Showing

Exhibiting a dog in the show ring sounds easy but, in fact, it entails a lot of training and preparation regardless of the breed. But, if you take a Lhasa Apso's long coat into consideration, you will really need to be dedicated. Keeping a Lhasa in full coat demands time, patience and skill.

Preparing this singular looking dog to look his best in the ring is an art in itself, and one which will take many years to perfect. In addition to show presentation, a Lhasa must learn how to cope with the busy show atmosphere.

You will need to work on his socialisation, and also take him to ringcraft classes so you both learn what is required in the ring. Your Lhasa will be subjected to a detailed 'hands on' examination by the judge; he must learn to stand still in a show pose and to move on a loose lead so the judge can assess his gait.

Showing at the top level is highly addictive, so watch out, once you start, you will never have a free date in your diary!

Dancing with dogs

This is a relatively new discipline and is growing in popularity, despite the hard work that is involved. Dog and handler perform a choreographed routine to music, allowing the dog to show off an array of tricks and moves, which delight the crowd.

There are two categories: heelwork to music where heelwork in different positions make up the larger percentage of the routine, and canine freestyle which allow the dog to work at a greater distance from the handler, and will include some of the more spectacular moves.

Both categories demand a huge amount of training but if you keep sessions light-hearted, with plenty of tasty food rewards on offer, the Lhasa will prove to be a real crowd-pleaser!

Health care

We are fortunate that the Lhasa Apso is a healthy breed and with good routine care, a well-balanced diet, and sufficient exercise, most will experience few health problems.

However, it is your responsibility to put a programme of preventative health care in place, and this should start from the moment your puppy, or older dog, arrives in his new home.

Vaccinations

Dogs are subject to a number of contagious diseases. In the old days, these were killers, and resulted in heartbreak for many owners. Vaccinations have now been developed, and the occurrence of the major infectious diseases is now very rare. However, this will only remain the case if all pet owners follow a strict policy of vaccinating their dogs. There are vaccinations available for the following diseases:

Adenovirus (Canine Adenovirus): This attacks the liver and affected dogs have a classic 'blue eye'.

Distemper: A viral disease which causes chest and gastro-intestinal damage. The brain may also be affected, leading to fits and paralysis.

Parvovirus: Causes severe gastroenteritis, and most commonly affects puppies.

Leptospirosis: This bacterial disease is carried by rats and affects many mammals, including humans. It causes liver and kidney damage.

Rabies: A virus that affects the nervous system and is invariably fatal. The first signs are abnormal behaviour when the infected dog may bite another animal or a person. Paralysis and death follow. Vaccination is compulsory in most countries. In the UK, dogs travelling overseas must be vaccinated.

Kennel cough: There are several strains of kennel cough, but they all result in a harsh, dry, cough. This disease is rarely fatal; in fact most dogs make a good recovery within a matter of weeks and show few signs of ill health while they are affected.

However, kennel cough is highly infectious among dogs that live together so, for this reason, most boarding kennels will insist that your dog is protected by the vaccine, which is given as nose drops.

Lyme disease: This is a bacterial disease transmitted by ticks. The first signs are limping, but the heart, kidneys and nervous system can also be affected.

The ticks that transmit the disease occur in specific regions, such as the north-east states of the USA, some of the southern states, California and the upper Mississippi region. Lyme disease is still rare in the UK so vaccinations are not routinely offered.

Vaccination programme

In the USA, the American Animal Hospital Association advises vaccination for core diseases, which they list as distemper, adenovirus, parvovirus and rabies.

The requirement for vaccinating for non-core diseases – leptospirosis, lyme disease and kennel cough – should be assessed depending on a dog's individual risk and his likely exposure to the disease. In the UK, vaccinations are routinely given for distemper, adenovirus, leptospirosis and parvovirus.

In most cases, a puppy will start his vaccinations at around eight weeks of age, with the second part given a fortnight later. However, this does vary depending on the individual policy of veterinary practices, and the incidence of disease in your area. You should also talk to your vet about whether to give annual booster vaccinations. This depends on an individual dog's levels of immunity, and how long a particular vaccine remains effective.

Parasites

No matter how well you look after your Lhasa Apso, you will have to accept that parasites (internal and external) are ever present, and you need to take preventative action.

Internal parasites: As the name suggests, these parasites live inside your dog. Most will find a home in the digestive tract, but there is also a parasite that lives in the heart. If infestation is unchecked, a dog's health will be severely jeopardised, but routine preventative treatment is simple and effective.

External parasites: These parasites live on your dog's body – in his skin and fur, and sometimes in his ears.

Roundworm

This is found in the small intestine, and signs of infestation will be a poor coat, a pot belly, diarrhoea and lethargy. Pregnant mothers should be treated, but it is almost inevitable that parasites will be passed on to the puppies.

For this reason, a breeder will start a worming programme, which you will need to continue. Ask your vet for advice on treatment, which will be on-going throughout your dog's life.

Tapeworm

Infection occurs when fleas and lice are ingested; the adult worm takes up residence in the small intestine, releasing mobile segments (which contain eggs) that can be seen in a dog's faeces as small rice-like grains. The only other obvious sign of infestation is irritation of the anus. Again, routine preventative treatment is required throughout your Lhasa Apso's life.

Heartworm

This parasite is transmitted by mosquitoes, and so will only occur where these insects thrive. A warm environment is needed for the parasite to develop, so it is more likely to be present in areas with a warm, humid climate.

However, it is found in all parts of the USA, although its prevalence does vary. At present, heartworm is rarely seen in the UK.

Heartworm live in the right side of the heart. Larvae can grow up to 14 inches (35.5cm) in length. A dog

with heartworm is at severe risk from heart failure, so preventative treatment, as advised by your vet, is essential. Dogs living in the USA should have regular blood tests to check for the presence of infection.

Lungworm

Lungworm, or *Angiostrongylus vasorum*, is a parasite that lives in the heart and major blood vessels supplying the lungs. It can cause many problems, such as breathing difficulties, blood-clotting problems, sickness and diarrhoea, seizures, and can be fatal.

The parasite is carried by slugs and snails, and the dog becomes infected when ingesting these, often accidentally when rummaging through undergrowth. Lungworm is not common, but it is on the increase and a responsible owner should be aware of it.

Fortunately, it is easily preventable and even affected dogs usually make a full recovery if treated early enough. Your vet will be able to advise you on the risks in your area and what form of treatment may be required.

Fleas

A dog may carry dog fleas, cat fleas, and even human fleas. The flea stays on the dog only long enough to have a blood meal and to breed, but its presence will result in itching and scratching. If your dog has an allergy to fleas, which is usually a reaction to the flea's saliva, he will scratch himself until he is raw.

Preventative treatment needs be administered on a routine basis; this can be in the form of a tablet, spot-on treatment, an insecticidal spray or shampoo. Ask your vet for advice on what product to use.

Bear in mind that the whole environment your dog lives in will need to be sprayed, and all other pets living in your home will also need to be treated.

How to detect fleas

You may suspect your dog has fleas, but how can you be sure? There are two methods to try.

Run a fine comb through your dog's coat, and see if you can detect the presence of fleas on the skin, or clinging to the comb. Alternatively, sit your dog on white paper and rub his back. This will dislodge faeces from the fleas, which will be visible as small brown specks. To double check, shake the specks on to damp cotton-wool. Flea faeces consists of the dried blood taken from the host, so if the specks turn a lighter shade of red, you know your dog has fleas.

Ticks

These are blood-sucking parasites which are most frequently found in rural areas where sheep or deer are present.

The main danger is their ability to pass Lyme disease to both dogs and humans. Lyme disease is prevalent in some areas of the USA, although it is still rare in the UK. The treatment you give your dog for fleas generally works for ticks, but you should discuss the best product to use with your vet.

How to remove a tick

If you spot a tick on your dog, do not try to pluck it off as you risk leaving the hard mouth parts embedded in his skin. The best way to remove a tick is to use a fine pair of tweezers, or you can buy a tick remover. Grasp the tick head firmly and then pull the tick straight out from the skin. If you are using a tick remover, check the instructions, as some recommend a circular twist when pulling. When you have removed the tick, clean the area with mild soap and water.

Ear mites

These parasites live in the outer ear canal. The signs of infestation are a brown, waxy discharge, and your dog will continually shake his head and scratch his ear.

If you suspect your Lhasa Apso has ear mites, a visit to the vet will be needed so that medicated ear drops can be prescribed.

Fur mites

These small, white parasites are visible to the naked eye and are often referred to as 'walking dandruff'. They cause a scurfy coat and mild itchiness. However, they are zoonetic – transferable to humans

– so prompt treatment with an insecticide prescribed by your vet is essential.

Harvest mites

These are picked up from the undergrowth, and can be seen as a bright orange patch on the webbing between the toes, although this can be found elsewhere on the body, such as on the ears flaps. Treatment is effective with the appropriate insecticide.

Skin mites

There are two types of parasite that burrow into a dog's skin. *Demodex canis* is transferred from a mother to her pups while they are feeding. Treatment is with a topical preparation, and sometimes antibiotics are needed.

The other skin mite, *Sarcoptes scabiei*, causes intense itching and hair loss. It is highly contagious, so all dogs in a household will need to be treated, which involves repeated bathing with a medicated shampoo.

Common ailments

As with all living animals, dogs can be affected by a variety of ailments. Most can be treated effectively after consulting with your vet, who will prescribe appropriate medication and will advise you on how to care for your dog's needs.

Here are some of the more common problems that could affect your Lhasa Apso, with advice on how to deal with them.

Anal glands

These are two small sacs on either side of the anus, which produce a dark-brown secretion that dogs use when they mark their territory.

The anal glands should empty every time a dog defecates but if they become blocked or impacted, a dog will experience increasing discomfort. He may nibble at his rear end, or scoot his bottom along the ground to relieve the irritation.

Treatment involves a trip to the vet, who will empty the glands manually. It is important to do this without delay or infection may occur.

Dental problems

Good dental hygiene will do much to minimise gum infection and tooth decay, which is why teeth cleaning should be part of your regular care routine.

If tartar accumulates to the extent that you cannot remove it by brushing, the vet will need to intervene. In a situation such as this, an anaesthetic will need to be administered so the tartar can be removed manually.

Diarrhoea

There are many reasons why a dog has diarrhoea, but most commonly it is the result of scavenging, a sudden change of diet, or an adverse reaction to a particular type of food.

If your dog is suffering from diarrhoea, the first step is to withdraw food for a day. It is important that he does not dehydrate, so make sure that fresh drinking water is available.

However, drinking too much can increase the diarrhoea, which may be accompanied by vomiting, so limit how much he drinks at any one time.

After allowing the stomach to rest, feed a bland diet, such as white fish or chicken with boiled rice, for a few days. In most cases, your dog's motions will return to normal and you can resume usual feeding, although this should be done gradually.

However, if this fails to work and the diarrhoea persists for more than a few days, you should consult you vet.

Your dog may have an infection which needs to be treated with antibiotics, or the diarrhoea may indicate some other problem which needs expert diagnosis.

Ear infections

The Lhasa Apso has drop ears, with abundant feathering which means that air cannot circulate freely, potentially creating an ideal environment for infection.

A healthy ear is clean with no sign of redness or inflammation, and no evidence of a waxy brown discharge or a foul odour. If you see your dog scratching his ear, shaking his head, or holding one ear at an odd angle, you will need to consult your vet.

The most likely causes are ear mites, an infection, or there may be a foreign body, such as a grass seed, trapped in the ear.

Depending on the cause, treatment is with medicated ear drops, possibly containing antibiotics. If a foreign body is suspected, the vet will need to carry out further investigations.

Eye problems

The Lhasa Apso has medium-sized eyes, which are neither sunken nor prominent. This lack of exaggeration means that a Lhasa's eyes should not be predisposed to infection or vulnerable to injury or trauma, which is the case with breeds such as the Pekingese, which have somewhat bulging eyes.

However, if your Lhasa Apso's eyes look red and

sore, he may be suffering from conjunctivitis. This may, or may not be accompanied with a watery or a crusty discharge.

Conjunctivitis can be caused by a bacterial or viral infection, it could be the result of an injury, or it could be an adverse reaction to pollen.

You will need to consult your vet for a correct diagnosis, but in the case of an infection, treatment with medicated eye drops is effective.

See Breed specific disorders

Foreign bodies

In the home, puppies – and some older dogs – cannot resist chewing anything that looks interesting. The toys you choose for your dog should be suitably robust to withstand damage, but children's toys can be irresistible.

Some dogs will chew – and swallow – anything from socks, tights, and any other items from the laundry basket to golf balls and stones from the garden. Obviously, these items are indigestible and could cause an obstruction in your dog's intestine, which is potentially lethal.

The signs to look for are vomiting, and a tucked up posture. The dog will often be restless and will look

as though he is in pain. In this situation, you must get your dog to the vet without delay, as surgery may be needed to remove the obstruction.

Heatstroke

The Lhasa Apso's head structure, with the short muzzle and flat nose, means that he is more likely to suffer from respiratory problems. He has a low tolerance to heat and can overheat quickly, resulting in excessive panting and some degree of stress.

If the weather is warm, make sure your Lhasa Apso has access to shady areas, and wait for a cooler part of the day before going for a walk.

Be extra careful if you leave your Lhasa in the car as the temperature can rise dramatically – even on a cloudy day. Heatstroke can happen very rapidly, and unless you are able to lower your dog's temperature, it can be fatal.

If your dog appears to be suffering from heatstroke, lie him flat and work at lowering his temperature by spraying him with cool water and covering him with wet towels.

As soon as he has made some recovery, take him to the vet, where cold intravenous fluids can be administered.

Lameness/ limping

There are a wide variety of reasons why a dog can go lame, from a simple muscle strain to a fracture, ligament damage, or more complex problems with the joints. If you are concerned about your dog, do not delay in seeking help.

As your Lhasa Apso becomes more elderly, he may suffer from arthritis, which you will see as general stiffness, particularly when he gets up after resting. It will help if you ensure his bed is in a warm draught-free location, and if your Lhasa gets wet after exercise, you must dry him thoroughly. If he seems to be in pain, consult your vet who will be able to help with pain relief medication.

Skin problems

If your dog is scratching or nibbling at his skin, first check he is free from fleas. There are other external parasites which cause itching and hair loss, but you will need a vet to help you find the culprit.

An allergic reaction is another major cause of skin problems. It can be quite an undertaking to find the cause of the allergy, and you will need to follow your vet's advice, which often requires eliminating specific ingredients from the diet, as well as looking at environmental factors. See Breed specific disorders

Breed-specific disorders

Like all pedigree dogs, the Lhasa Apso does have some breed-related disorders. If diagnosed with any of the diseases listed here, it is important to remember that they can affect offspring so breeding from such dogs should be discouraged.

There are now recognised screening tests to enable breeders to check for affected individuals and hence reduce the prevalence of these diseases within the breed.

DNA testing is also becoming more widely available, and as research into the different genetic diseases progresses, more DNA tests are being developed.

Eye disorders

Cataract

Cataracts are an opacification of the lens that tends to occur in older dogs. There are varying degrees of severity, with the inherited form often having little effect on eyesight but, if necessary, surgery is usually a successful treatment.

Screening is available for this condition.

Entropion

This is an inherited eye condition which presents as an in-rolling of the eyelids.

This ranges in severity from mild to the more serious, where surgical correction is required because of the pain and damage that is inflicted on the eyeball.

Keratoconjunctivitis sicca

Also known as 'dry eye', this is caused by inadequate tear production. Initially the eyes look sore and red, with a discharge; the cornea may become clouded, ultimately resulting in loss of vision. Medication to keep the eyes lubricated is effective but treatment is on-going for the duration of the dog's life.

Progressive Retinal Atrophy (PRA)

This condition involves the destruction of the photoreceptors in the retina. As the disease progresses the retina shrivels up resulting in total loss of vision. The onset of PRA can be between two and eight years of age. All breeding stock should be screened for this condition.

Haemophilia

This affects the ability of the blood to clot; the inheritance pattern is sex-linked which means that females are carriers and males are either affected or clear. There is no cure but the condition can be managed with vigilance. Blood transfusions may be necessary if the dog suffers a bleeding episode.

Renal Dysplasia

A malformation of the kidneys has a devastating effect, which means the affected puppy fails to grow and thrive. It is commonly diagnosed within the first few months but some dogs may not show signs until they are four or five years of age. Weight loss, lethargy, vomiting and collapse occur in the later stages.

Skin disorders

As already highlighted, skin problems can be the result of parasites or an allergy, but they can also be inherited and linked to an underlying allergy. Effects can range from recurrent skin infections to compulsive licking of paws, resulting in pink discolouration, and incessant itching.

Congenital Hypotrichosis

This condition arises when there is abnormal development of the hair follicles. Apparent, from birth, or within the first few weeks, there is a permanent absence of hair which cannot be rectified. It may be confined to the top of the head, it may affect the whole head, including ears, plus abdomen, and in severe cases it may affect the legs and tail.

The health of the individual is not affected, but the condition needs to be managed by using medicated shampoos, prescribed by the vet, and avoiding extremes of temperature.

Sebaceous adentis

The Lhasa Apso is predisposed to this condition which is caused by the inflammation of the sebaceous glands which are being attacked by the immune system.

The first signs are a fine, silvery dandruff progressing to alopecia (baldness) starting from the head and ears, advancing to the neck and back.

Recurrent skin infections are common. It can be treated with shampoos and supplementing the diet with fatty acids. Antibiotics will be needed for skin infections, and if the dog becomes resistant to these, euthanasia may be the only option.

Urioliths

This occurs where stones or excessive amounts of crystals form within the urinary tract. These irritate the lining, resulting in pain and blood in the urine. Secondary bacterial infections are not uncommon. Diet is strongly implicated in this condition so changing diet can have a beneficial effect.

Summing up

It may give the pet owner cause for concern to find out about health problems that may affect their dog. But it is important to bear in mind that acquiring some basic knowledge is an asset, as it will allow you to spot signs of trouble at an early stage. Early diagnosis is very often the means to the most effective treatment. Fortunately, the Lhasa Apso is a generally healthy and disease-free dog, with his only visits to the vet being annual check-ups. In most cases, owners can look forward to enjoying many happy years with this affectionate and highly entertaining companion.

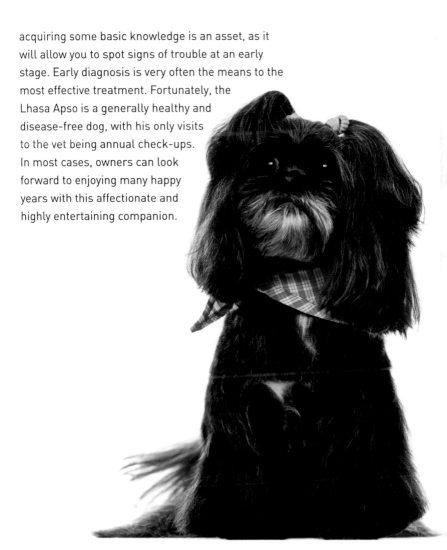

Useful addresses

Breed & Kennel Clubs
Please contact your Kennel Club to obtain contact information about breed clubs in your area.

UK
The Kennel Club (UK)
1 Clarges Street London, W1J 8AB
Telephone: 0870 606 6750
Fax: 0207 518 1058
Web: www.thekennelclub.org.uk

USA
American Kennel Club (AKC)
5580 Centerview Drive, Raleigh, NC 27606.
Telephone: 919 233 9767
Fax: 919 233 3627
Email: info@akc.org
Web: www.akc.org

United Kennel Club (UKC)
100 E Kilgore Rd, Kalamazoo,
MI 49002-5584, USA.
Tel: 269 343 9020
Fax: 269 343 7037
Web:www.ukcdogs.com

Australia
Australian National Kennel Council (ANKC)
The Australian National Kennel Council is the administrative body for pure breed canine affairs in Australia. It does not, however, deal directly with dog exhibitors, breeders or judges. For information pertaining to breeders, clubs or shows, please contact the relevant State or Territory Body.

International
Fédération Cynologique Internationalé (FCI)
Place Albert 1er, 13, B-6530 Thuin, Belgium.
Tel: +32 71 59.12.38
Fax: +32 71 59.22.29
Web: www.fci.be

Training and behavior
UK
Association of Pet Dog Trainers
Telephone: 01285 810811
Web: www.apdt.co.uk

Canine Behaviour
Association of Pet Behaviour Counsellors
Telephone: 01386 751151
Web: www.apbc.org.uk

USA
Association of Pet Dog Trainers
Tel: 1 800 738 3647
Web: www.apdt.com

American College of Veterinary Behaviorists
Web: www.dacvb.org

American Veterinary Society of Animal Behavior
Web: www.avsabonline.org

Australia
APDT Australia Inc
Web: www.apdt.com.au

For details of regional behaviorists, contact the relevant State or Territory Controlling Body.

Activities

UK

Agility Club
www.agilityclub.co.uk

British Flyball Association
Telephone: 01628 829623
Web: www.flyball.org.uk

USA

North American Dog Agility Council
Web: www.nadac.com

North American Flyball Association, Inc.
Tel/Fax: 800 318 6312
Web: www.flyball.org

Australia

Agility Dog Association of Australia
Tel: 0423 138 914
Web: www.adaa.com.au

NADAC Australia
Web: www.nadacaustralia.com

Australian Flyball Association
Tel: 0407 337 939
Web: www.flyball.org.au

International

World Canine Freestyle Organisation
Tel: (718) 332-8336
Web: www.worldcaninefreestyle.org

Health

UK

British Small Animal Veterinary Association
Tel: 01452 726700
Web: www.bsava.com

Royal College of Veterinary Surgeons
Tel: 0207 222 2001
Web: www.rcvs.org.uk

Alternative Veterinary Medicine Centre
Tel: 01367 710324
Web: www.alternativevet.org

USA

American Veterinary Medical Association
Tel: 800 248 2862
Web: www.avma.org

American College of Veterinary Surgeons
Tel: 301 916 0200
Toll Free: 877 217 2287
Web: www.acvs.org

Canine Eye Registration Foundation
The Veterinary Medical DataBases
1717 Philo Rd, PO Box 3007,
Urbana, IL 61803-3007
Tel: 217-693-4800
Fax: 217-693-4801
Web: www.vmdb.org/cerf

Orthopaedic Foundation of Animals
2300 E Nifong Boulevard
Columbia, Missouri, 65201-3806
Tel: 573 442-0418
Fax: 573 875-5073
Web: www.offa.org

American Holistic Veterinary Medical
Association
Tel: 410 569 0795
Web: www.ahvma.org

Australia

Australian Small Animal Veterinary
Association
Tel: 02 9431 5090
Web: www.asava.com.au

Australian Veterinary Association
Tel: 02 9431 5000
Web: www.ava.com.au

Australian College Veterinary Scientists
Tel: 07 3423 2016
Web: www.acvsc.org.au

Australian Holistic Vets
Web: www.ahv.com.au